All
about
house
plants

All about house plants

William Davidson

Spring Books

London · New York · Sydney · Toronto

First published in 1974 by
The Hamlyn Publishing Group Limited

This edition published in 1983 by
Spring Books
Astronaut House, Feltham, Middlesex, England

ISBN 0 600 38538 8

Printed in Hong Kong

nooooolo3567wo6605co3838k20128

Contents

Aphelandra squarrosa Brockfeld

Colour illustrations

Fittonia verschaffeltii

Making the most of house plants

We acquire knowledge of plants in many and varied ways: by paying attention at school, listening to others expound on the subject, or by practical participation in growing them. All these sources of knowledge can, no doubt, solve many problems but, to my mind, the best way to learn about the everyday problems of plant growing is to be responsible for a plant display at any major flower show. There you will hear astonishing tales about success and failure, and some of the incredible things that can happen to a humble rubber plant or sansevieria.

My job takes me to many such flower shows, and requires me to answer a vast number of letters on the subject of indoor plants. Some letters are amusing, others quite sad; some concern premature loss of leaves while others are from perplexed householders who have room ceilings too low for rampant monstera plants.

Between show attendances and letter answering a somewhat unique knowledge of plants has been acquired – much of it useless, but a great deal closely concerned with plants and the problems they present for the average householder. It is hoped in the ensuing pages that the reader will benefit from the worthwhile information and be amused by the more bizarre incidents.

Talking to members of flower arrangement and gardening clubs, and listening to their many questions at the close of proceedings, can also be helpful in building up a knowledge of plants. Particularly so when a member describes how successful he has been with growing *Begonia rex*, for instance, or stephanotis, and gives an account of how the plant is cared for. In this way you really do learn about success and failure, and how to improve your chances of growing bigger and better plants indoors.

Of all the many points that come to light during these discussions it is abundantly clear that plants grown in good light do very much better than those which struggle along in a dark corner. Good light should not be confused with bright sunlight – too much of the latter can be damaging to the majority of plants used for indoor decoration. To make the most of house plants adequate light is essential, particularly in respect of plants with variegated foliage.

In the light, airy room that affords a constant temperature throughout the year there is an endless range of plants to choose from which will soften and improve the surroundings. Although a note can be taken of particular plants which are suited to particular situations, given reasonable conditions the majority of plants, other than known tender ones, will do well. This is borne out if one visits the home of the dedicated house plant expert. He, or more often she, will have plants in every room in the house, from the loo to the larder. In such homes one is quite concerned on performing the simplest movement for fear of knocking some treasured cryptanthus from its precarious perch. The home of the expert does help to prove, however, that room plants can be reared almost anywhere in the house where conditions are reasonable.

The entrance hall is often the most suitable place for an effective grouping of plants, or for the more mature individual plant. It is the first place that the visitor steps into and there is much to be said for the warm welcome that a cheerful entrance hall can provide. Conditions are often cooler here, though, so one must choose plants carefully to ensure that they are not too delicate and will tolerate the lower temperatures that are likely to prevail. Many suitable plants will be found in the A to Z chapter which, among other requirements, gives details of temperatures needed by the various plants in order to give the best results.

Most flowering plants do better in a light, cool hallway than in a stuffy room, and the hydrangea is no exception

The ivies, of which there are many different varieties, often prove to be ideal for the entrance hall; in particular the larger leaved ones such as *Hedera canariensis*, *H. Goldleaf* and *H. maculata*. These will all look better if the growth can be trained to a fan-shaped support of some kind. Trellis work is ideal and can be attached to the wall, or a fan-shaped framework can be simply made by inserting two stout canes in the plant pot and joining them at intervals with shorter pieces of cane some 18 in. long.

This will provide an excellent framework on which old plant growth can be trained by hand, and on which new growth can twine naturally as it develops.

The kangaroo vine, *Cissus antarctica*, is another plant that will attain fairly large proportions in time and will enjoy a cooler position in which to grow. In very hot rooms *C. antarctica* quite quickly develops dry, brown leaves and is eventually reduced to a cluster of unattractive leafless stems. Providing a

Ivies are ideal for the entrance hall, particularly the large-leaved ones such as *Hedera canariensis* (left) and *Hedera Goldleaf* (right). Also illustrated is *Hedera helix cristata*

framework for the growth of the kangaroo vine to cling to also sets off the pleasant green leaves of this Australian native to best advantage.

In the entrance hall draughts can present problems, so some precautions should be taken to protect plants by fitting draught excluders. Occasional opening of the front door is not so harmful provided it is not left open for long periods during cold spells. A cold, cutting draught will quickly prove fatal to the majority of foliage plants. Where the staircase leads off directly from the hall a bamboo or similar framework following the line of the staircase provides an excellent support for climbing plants. The pots in which the plants are growing can be tucked away out of sight under the staircase where they will cause much less obstruction. Although it is essential that the plant growth should enjoy reasonable light in which to grow, the same does not apply to the pot in which the plant is growing. However, some plantsmen may object and say that concealing the pots gives the overall display an artificial appearance, but this is purely a matter of personal taste.

The majority of flowering pot plants will do much better in the lighter and cooler hallway – certainly in these conditions they will remain in flower and give pleasure for a much longer period than in a stuffy room. Cyclamen, azaleas, hydrangeas and primulas would give an infinitely better account of themselves. In very hot conditions the cyclamen can prove to be extremely difficult, and azaleas will come into full flower and pass their best much more rapidly.

As mentioned earlier, the real enthusiast will utilise every corner of the house in order to grow the maximum number of plants. So they are everywhere, but for the life of me I cannot see what advantage there is in having the bedroom filled with plants. My view is that one should have plants in rooms that are used most frequently, where they can be enjoyed to the full. Yet I can think of one customer who calls at the nursery annually to purchase a considerable number of pot plants for his home, and each time he brings in his treasured *Anthurium scherzerianum* for its yearly overhaul. This is very much a bedroom plant as far as the customer is concerned. When he first brought it in we were inquisitive to know what the fine layer of white dust on the leaves could be. We soon discovered that it was talcum powder which, if anything, seemed to improve rather than mar the plant's performance, though it did not exactly improve its appearance!

Even the simplest flower arrangement is the better for having a focal point to attract the eye, which is usually in the form of an unusual or particularly fine flower. The rest of the arrangement is complementary to the centre piece. The same may be said of the plant arrangement with a fine cryptanthus or similarly unusual plant as a centre piece. We have focal points in our rooms; it may be a television set, a fine piece of furniture, or a striking flower arrangement. In the same way an interesting group of plants may be used as a central feature.

Plants grouped together are infinitely more effective than an equivalent number of plants dotted about the room. A collection of poor

Lovely as they are, cyclamen can be difficult to please, disliking hot, dry conditions. This is one of the strain known as Silver Leaf

plants are better displayed as a group, concealing many of their defects, rather than standing around as leafless and tattered individuals.

Part of my job is to be responsible for staging plant displays at flower shows, exhibitions and garden centres around the country. It is amazing to see the number of plants with only a few leaves at the top which can be hidden away in a group in an exhibit. Only the top of the plant is seen by the onlooker, and the overall effect is often surprisingly good, though one cannot help feeling that there is something unethical about this form of presentation. Our aim when exhibiting is to show each plant on its individual merit, so they are spaced accordingly. However, this is simplified by the fact that there are a vast number of plants to choose from when building up a display, from the lowly *Ficus pumila* to more majestic plants in the same family, such as *F. lyrata, benjamina* and *benghalensis*.

Indoor plants cannot be expected to grow as lushly and well as they do in temperature- and light-controlled greenhouses where moisture requirements are as near ideal as can possibly be expected, so it would seem almost inevitable that at least a percentage of any collection of plants growing indoors will be some way below perfection. And it would be hopelessly uneconomical to suggest that the householder should immediately discard plants that have shed a leaf or two and go out and purchase replacements. Therefore, it can be assumed that unless one is an expert with veritably ideal conditions, almost every collection of indoor plants will contain at least a few inferior ones.

In order to set these off to better advantage the possibility of grouping plants together in trays or troughs may well be considered. Much will depend on the size of the room in which plants are being displayed, but it will be found that an infinite variety of containers specially made for housing plants can be purchased quite easily. Or the handyman with little more than average ability can construct simple display boxes or troughs. It will be important to ensure that the container is watertight.

Many of the photographs contained in these pages will give the reader some indication of what is needed when arranging a display of plants indoors. It is difficult to lay down definite rules because the plants themselves vary so much. The writer, when offering advice, may have in mind a perfect specimen of a rubber plant glowing with good health while the reader, on the other hand, may be faced with what can equally well be described as a rubber plant, but it may, in fact, have only a few leaves at the top of an otherwise bare stem. The method employed in displaying two such plants would vary considerably. Then again, people are very variable – some have natural artistic ability, others may be taught how to arrange things artistically, while an unfortunate few remain quite incapable of expressing themselves artistically regardless of the amount of instruction they have had.

Having an artistic bent also helps when plants are being purchased. It often saddens me to see a purchaser select the least attractive plant from a batch on display simply because they are unable to appreciate fully the merits of respective plants. And one cannot stress too often the importance of purchasing good quality plants at the outset; the inferior plant cannot possibly be expected to do so well when introduced to indoor conditions.

Fortunately, there is an ample range of indoor plants from which to choose, so it is not difficult to create a wide variety of differing effects, and this can often be done by simply rearranging the same plants. Many of the plants will fit into almost any colour scheme, while others require selection and placing with some care. The plants with harder red colouring, such as crotons, poinsettias and *Dracaena terminalis*,

are possibly the most difficult to incorporate in a display; my tendency with these is to provide a background of greenery against which the more difficult colours are easier on the eye.

Some plants are almost essential when planning a larger display or arrangement. Following a talk on indoor plants I was once taken out of my stride when a questioner asked something that was not included in what I would term the standard questions. The questioner wanted to know what my ten favourite house plants were. After thinking for a moment I gave him my answer, and it struck me that the plants I mentioned were in fact my ten favourite display plants – the ones without which I would feel rather lost in an exhibition hall or flower show marquee.

First on the list, though not necessarily the most important, was that graceful plant of the *Araliaceae* family, *Aralia elegantissima*, known as *Dizygotheca elegantissima*, which is a much less manageable name for the average person to cope with. *A. elegantissima* has graceful foliage which is nearly black in really healthy plants, and can be included in almost any grouping and not be out of place. However, as this plant ages coarser leaves develop and it loses much of its earlier attraction, but it takes many years for this change to take place and should not discourage one from purchasing young plants.

For bolder displays the monstera must surely find a place, and far and away the most suitable subject for underplanting an imposing monstera plant is the red-centred bromeliad, *Neoregelia carolinae tricolor*, which is another of my favourite top ten display plants. Another plant that is difficult to better when it comes to filling darker areas under larger plants is the bird's nest fern, *Asplenium nidus*. The leaves, arranged in the form of a shuttlecock, are of the palest green colouring and require little skill to set them off to best effect.

At opposite ends of the size scale are two members of the fig family. The fiddle-leaved fig, *Ficus lyrata*, is an especially fine and majestic plant which is frequently seen as the principal feature of large displays of indoor plants. The smaller plant is the creeping fig, *F. pumila* which, as the common name suggests, creeps along the ground and is ideal for finishing off displays and arrangements. Really, the figs do play a most important part in our work and it is difficult to omit the graceful form of the weeping fig, *F. benjamina*, from the top ten.

As with cacti, there is a firm division of opinion concerning *Sansevieria trifasciata laurentii*, mother-in-law's tongue; you either like them or you don't. For me mother-in-law must be included here, not because she is incredibly tough almost to the point of being indestructible, but also because she is very useful for providing a display with a change of leaf form. Also, the greenish-yellow colouring is complementary to many of the other plants in the house plant range. Although I have no particular preference, as a group of plants the *Dracaena deremensis* types have much to commend them; mostly grey and white in colour they invariably give one's plant arrangements a touch of the exotic with their broad, boldly striped leaves.

Another green plant, *Schefflera actinophylla*, can take on really superb proportions when well grown. Most plants when grown in pots will have one aspect that is more pleasing to the eye than any other, and that is why we often stand back from the display and get a colleague to rotate the plant pot gently so that the most desirable view can be presented to onlookers. This rule, however, does not always apply to the schefflera which is very much an individual sort of plant that can be viewed with equally good effect from all angles. This is also one of the principal reasons for its popularity as an office landscaping plant. Solitary specimens

of this kind in an attractive container can frequently be much more impressive than the same container filled with a motley collection of lesser plants.

It will be noted that the majority of the foregoing plants are capable of developing into fairly large specimens in time and will form the backbone of most displays. There are many other equally suitable plants, and one cannot really omit the crotons which are essential on account of their bright colouring of almost every hue which will improve the appearance of almost any display of purely foliage plants.

Over the years I have developed a very deep attachment for plants and can at different times find uses for almost all the many varieties when preparing displays or suggesting plantings. Choosing ten plants which I really disliked would present me with much more of a poser than selecting my ten favourites.

Sometimes indoors a portable display can have advantages over a static one – the mobile display can be placed in a light window position during the day and moved into a warmer area of the room at other times. Such a display would be

A bowl of mixed plants makes an attractive focal point in a room. Included here, from left to right, are *Calathea zebrina*, *Fatshedera lizei*, *Dizygotheca elegantissima*, *Begonia serratifolia*, and the trailing stems of *Ficus radicans variegata*

An indispensable
addition to any display
is the graceful
*Dizygotheca
elegantissima*, with its
almost black, fine-
toothed leaves

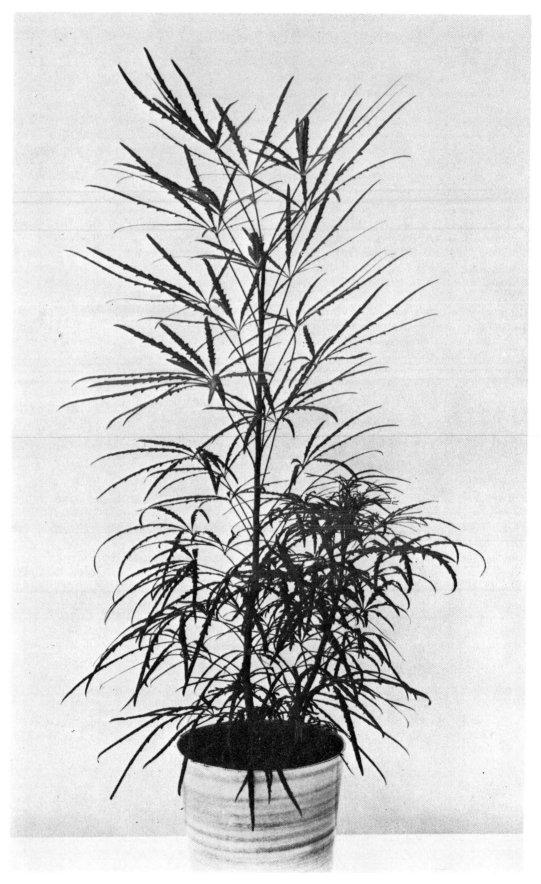

Some larger plants can have an impressive effect when grouped together. On the floor are *Aralia sieboldii* and *Azalea indica* with *Aglaonema pseudo-bracteatum* and *Pandanus veitchii* on the table

more suitable for smaller plants which are easier to handle and come to less harm when being moved around. And an excellent basis for a display of this kind is an old tea trolley, on which a tray can be placed for accommodating the plants. An inch or two of wet gravel on the tray, on which the pots may be placed, will greatly improve the plants' performance. It would not, however, be wise to move plants about to too many different locations as they do very much better once they have become adjusted to a particular environment, and can remain there. Being mobile there is also the added advantage of being able to take plants into the kitchen, or out of doors for that matter, in order to attend to maintenance, watering, feeding and so on. Need it be added that plants should not be taken out of doors on cold days, as a sudden temperature change even for a short period can be particularly damaging. This is another reason why one should purchase plants from a retailer who has heated premises, and insist on plants being properly wrapped and protected before taking them out of the shop.

The disused fireplace is another room feature that provides an excellent location for many of the indoor plants which are not too demanding in respect of light requirements. With central heating many fireplaces are never used and the less attractive ones are in time removed completely, but some of the more stylish remain as attractive features in the room. Using this area is not simply a matter of cleaning out the remains of the last fire and then arranging a show of plants. An important step is to ensure that the chimney vent is blocked off to minimise the possibility of draughts which will damage the plants. Also, in order to compensate for the generally poorer light around the fireplace area, it is often wise to install some form of lighting which will not only be beneficial to plant growth but will greatly enhance the appearance of the plants.

Strip lights are best as they give better coverage over the area occupied by plants, but whatever type of lighting is used it is important to ensure that the lights are sufficiently far from the plants to prevent them being scorched. This is particularly important in respect of spot lights which generate considerably more heat. In a book of this kind it is difficult to offer specific advice on the most suitable types of lighting as lights are forever being improved. It is better to consult the local electrical shop at the time lights are required so that the most up-to-date advice and fittings may be acquired.

Plant care

We seem to have come a long way with indoor plants in the last quarter of a century as plants in an ever-increasing variety are produced in their millions annually for an eager and interested public.

Often I am asked whether I foresee any fall-off in demand, but my optimism is as boundless as ever. The more houses that are built, the more mammoth office blocks that appear on the horizon, then the greater will be the potential for decorative indoor plants.

At one time there was only the cottage window providing a home for a cluster of comparatively uninteresting plants – these seldom got away from the fern, tradescantia and aspidistra. Nowadays, however, the scope has increased tremendously; with homes that are light, airy and well heated there seems to be no limit to the range of plants, both easy and delicate, that can be managed quite satisfactorily indoors. The general paraphernalia connected with plant culture indoors has kept step with increased world sales of plants. We now have an incredible assortment of simple and sophisticated, expensive and less expensive containers to choose from in which to accommodate our plants. Fertilisers, leaf-cleaning agents, self-watering gadgets – there is an infinite variety, but one should not be brainwashed into believing that an expensive range of equipment is necessary in order to be a successful indoor plant grower, though these things may help.

Often the reverse is the case: the plant owner who has little more than an old teapot with which to water his plants may be the most successful plant grower in the neighbourhood. And to add to the consternation, it will often be found that he fervently believes that cold tea is ideal for watering his plants – and his plants will often cause one to feel grudgingly that perhaps he has a point!

So, at the outset, it is emphasised that expensive equipment is not everything, as many a budding angler or golfer with money to burn has found to his cost. The bent pin in the hands of someone with natural ability can have its advantages! Natural ability is probably the best way of explaining the popular term 'green fingers' which seems to have an aura of mystique about it. But wherever you hear of the green-fingered ability of someone who grows all the plants in the book with consummate ease it will often be found that they invariably provide almost ideal conditions for plants. The consequence is that by growing healthy plants it is a simple matter to provide perfect material for cuttings for propagation. It is then very natural that a reputation for green fingers should develop, as almost everything seems to sprout roots as soon as the cutting is pointed at the compost.

Buying Your Plants

The provision of ideal conditions is not everything. Initially, it is essential to ensure that the plants one purchases are clean and healthy with a bit of sparkle to them. With so many plant suppliers eager to make a sale there is no need to purchase the first bedraggled plant that is encountered. Far better to shop around and find the shop or garden centre that offers quality plants, as these in themselves are an indication that the supplier knows a thing or two about green fingers as well.

Also, when you purchase a plant don't be too shy to ask for some advice on its culture, as you are likely to learn a great deal more from the raiser of the plant than you are ever likely to learn from a book. The grower may complain to his colleagues that with every plant he sells he has to give in advice and time what amounts to about half the value of the plant. But, take it from me, most of them, provided they have the time, enjoy being given the opportunity of discoursing at length on what, after all, is their pet subject.

It will often save possible disappointment if the salesman is consulted before any major plants are purchased – one can afford to experiment with the smaller and less expensive plants. Explain to the salesman the conditions in which you wish to grow particular plants and he will be able to recommend the kinds that are most likely to succeed. The wise salesman does not encourage his customer to purchase plants that are totally unsuited to the conditions the customer can provide; this will only lead to the bedraggled plant being returned soon after with the customer requesting a replacement.

When purchasing one must be practical and realise that, on the whole, plants do not grow very fast in room conditions. So, if you have a large room that needs a bold, mature plant in order to do a position justice then go out and buy a bold, mature plant. It is pointless to purchase a minute plant in a small pot and then ask the supplier how quickly it will grow. In ideal greenhouse conditions it may add 2 ft. each year and the nurseryman may say so. So you may purchase your plant in a small pot and a couple of 6-ft. bamboo canes on which to train the expected rampant growth when, in fact, the sight of these canes pushed into the small pot beside the equally tiny plant is enough to put it off growing altogether. Agreed, there are the odd few plants that settle down and grow quite rapidly, but on the whole plant growth indoors can seldom be described as vigorous.

Containers

Often the pot in which the plant is growing will influence the customer, and there is still a decided aversion to plastic pots among amateur and professional plant growers. So much so that the possibility of immediately transferring the plant from its plastic pot to one made of earthenware is often considered. Of course, there is no reason why this should not be done, provided the root ball is a good fit for the new pot – this may entail the use of a little extra compost to fill out any gaps. These days the commercial grower tends to favour the cheaper plastic which has many advantages over the clay pot in respect of handling, freight costs and use on capillary-watered greenhouse benches, where the many holes and the thin base of the plastic pot ensures that there is direct contact between the compost in the pot and the wet sand bed it stands on.

However, in our heart of hearts many of us professional nurserymen still have a slight bias in favour of the clay pot when it comes to caring for plants that are just that little bit more difficult to manage. The great advantage with clay pots indoors is that they do not retain moisture as long as the non-porous plastic, which reduces the possibility of plants dying from the effects of waterlogged conditions. Waterlogging, in my experience, is responsible for the failure of more indoor plants than any other single cause.

Whatever the type of pot, it is usually better to place it in a more decorative outer pot cover to improve the general appearance.

Group Planting

Besides covers for the individual pots, all sorts of troughs and bowls can be purchased for

Decorative watering-cans are among the many useful pieces of equipment available to the house plant enthusiast

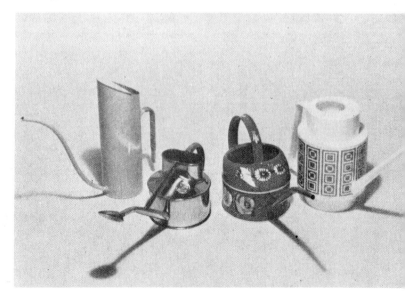

growing plants in a group. These to my mind are by far the best purchase, as there is little doubt that plants do very much better if grown in the company of other plants. When taking my first steps, as it were, into the mysteries of growing pot plants a hardened old nurseryman once informed me that his plants did very much better when grown in a group. At the time I suppose an amused smile creased my face, but since then the sight of poorly plants making an indifferent job of growing in splendid isolation has given me cause to recall his remark with less amusement.

Grouped together plants create a certain amount of humidity and feeling around one another, and this is a very important requirement in hot and dry room conditions. In the greenhouse we can combat the dry atmosphere created by the heating pipes by frequent damping of the area around the plants, and by wetting the ground beneath the staging and the pathways as frequently as possible. This damping down operation may take place several times daily, yet it may not be necessary to water the compost in which the plants are actually growing. If the compost is watered each time the greenhouse is damped down the soil will become totally saturated, depriving the roots of oxygen, a con-

dition which few plants can tolerate for long.

However, we cannot be expected to damp down the carpet, window-sills and floor area surrounding plants indoors, so there must be an alternative, and our larger container holding several plants provides that. Whatever sort of container is used it is important to ensure that it is watertight. Shallow trays can also be useful, with an inch or two of gravel in the bottom on which plant pots are stood. Keeping the gravel permanently moist will ensure that there is a certain amount of essential humidity around the plants, but it is important that, though the gravel is wet, the plant pots must at no time actually be standing in water as this will inevitably result in waterlogged soil conditions.

A second method is to employ a deeper container filled with moist peat. Plants do particularly well in such containers if the pot is plunged to the rim in the peat. The individual requirements of each plant can then be checked. By keeping the peat moist it will be found that the plants do not require to be watered as often as those placed individually on the window ledge. However, having emphasised the need for keeping the peat moist one must add a word of warning against overdoing it, as plants cannot

Plants thrive best in the company of others, but for a bowl arrangement it is important to ensure that they are compatible in their moisture requirements

possibly be expected to do well in the soggy mess that will result from too frequent watering. It is not unusual to find, on being asked to inspect a sickly collection of plants in the ideal type of peat-filled trough, that the plants are almost awash in a container filled nearly to the brim with water. Yet the concerned owner seems quite oblivious of the damage that is being done. Remember, the recommendation is that the peat should be kept moist, not saturated.

A third method of growing plants in a container is to fill the box or trough with a standard house plant potting compost and, removing the plants from their pots, plant them up more or less permanently in the mixture. To simplify the operation it is wise to arrange the plants in their probable positions on top of the compost before doing the planting. Very few of the larger containers are equipped with drainage holes in the base, so it is of the utmost importance to ensure that it is not overwatered. When adopting this method it is important to choose plants for grouping together which are reasonably compatible in their moisture requirements, as they will all have to suffer or enjoy the same conditions. For example, the moisture-loving cyperus would not be expected to do particularly

well in the same container as a sansevieria which prefers very much dryer root conditions.

Recent years have seen an astonishing increase in the number of attractively planted containers of mixed plants that are offered for sale, particularly at peak selling times such as Christmas. These containers, usually holding anything from five to ten plants, seldom have drainage holes in the bottom, and the planting will have been done with little thought for the compatibility of plants. When watering such plantings the tendency should always be to err on the side of dryness. Mixed plantings of this kind will remain reasonably attractive for anything up to one year from the time the arrangement is acquired. The plants can then be potted up individually, and some of the smaller plants used to replant the container.

Sphagnum Moss

Before leaving the subject of group planting sphagnum moss should be mentioned as a possible plunging material. Moss of this kind has many advantages, not least the fact that it is light, clean and easy to handle, and that difficult plants seem to do particularly well when plunged in it. Recalling my personal experience with the

Hedera, peperomia, *Scindapsus aureus*, tradescantia, *Cissus antarctica*, senecio and a saintpaulia grouped on a shallow, gravel-filled tray. By keeping the gravel moist, humidity is maintained around the leaves

success of a difficult plant may help to emphasise the advantages of this material.

There are many beautiful dieffenbachias available, the majority of which are a little difficult to care for; *Dieffenbachia* Pia can be among the most troublesome. The main difficulty is that the leaves contain very little chlorophyll, being almost entirely creamy white in colour. This in itself makes it a very fine plant for exhibition work, and it is especially useful and attractive when incorporated with blue saintpaulias. On the nursery no one was very keen to be given charge of greenhouses containing *D.* Pia, as the chances of success were not particularly good.

Purely by chance we discovered the best way to grow this plant when a container, measuring some 3 ft. across, was filled with sphagnum moss into which plants of *D.* Pia were plunged to their pot rims before being taken to a minor show. Containers filled in this way with one sort of plant can often be much more effective than a collection of assorted plants in the same sized container. Anyway, the large bowl of plants came back from the show and, instead of adopting the usual practice of dismantling the arrangement, we left it intact and placed it in a warm greenhouse.

The result was startling. Some two years later the previously delicate plants had grown apace and, in fact, no plant had so much as lost a leaf in spite of the very close planting. These dieffenbachias went on growing and in time reached their maximum height of some 3 ft. 6 in. Thereafter they produced young plants at the base of the parent stem and the original plant gradually deteriorated, which is common to all the dieffenbachias that are likely to be grown in a pot.

Since then we have raised many delicate plants equally well by using the same material for plunging pots. Filled with moss instead of peat or compost, containers are much lighter and easier to handle, and there is little chance of the moss becoming excessively wet. Indoors, containers some 15 in. in diameter and about 5 in. in depth can be filled with moss and a collection of five or six plants used to give a very pleasing effect. There is also the added advantage when using moss that the plants can be rearranged with little trouble and new designs can be made almost on the instant, often with the same plants. One hesitates to make any sort of guarantee concerning the possible life of plants indoors, but it can be said that by employing sphagnum moss as a plunging material the least green-fingered house plant grower will achieve results that previously seemed quite beyond him.

One simple precaution: the moss should not be left in the container too long undisturbed, as it tends to become sour in time and the subsequent odour can be less than pleasant! The best plan is to remove the moss from the container every two or three months out of doors, and allow the air to get at it for a little while before replacing. When planted up the moss should be kept moist and the plants watered individually as required.

Acquiring moss can sometimes present a problem, particularly in the city. In these circumstances it is usually best to visit the florist and explain what the moss is required for; it may also help if one or two plants are purchased at the same time!

There are, of course, other ways of acquiring moss and my experience of doing just this in Killarney some years ago has always remained with me. When asked to stage a plant display at a florist's conference I made what I thought were ideal arrangements for transportation of plants from the United Kingdom and provision of moss from a contact in Dublin for setting up the display.

The plants had a somewhat hazardous 200-mile journey by private motor coach from Dublin with a number of conference delegates. In typical Irish fashion the coach developed a habit of stopping at almost every ale house en route; the plants suffered a little, those in charge more than a little and the carefully arranged sphagnum moss disappeared altogether. Needless to say, the coach, due to arrive at midday, trundled into the hotel forecourt in Killarney in carnival mood nearer midnight.

Next day, we were in serious bother until Michael, the local florist, learned of our predicament, got in his car and offered to lead us to an abundance of moss. This entailed a hair-raising journey up miles of mountain track at breakneck speed on a road designed for a leisurely Irish donkey. Michael then stopped his car and said, 'There you are, you will get all the moss you want here.' Sure enough, we had seen moss growing on many a Scottish hillside, but nothing to compare with these enormous mounds of spongy moss in the most beautiful colours that one could possibly imagine. The display was duly completed but the florists, to my consternation, were much more interested in the source of the superb sphagnum moss than they were in the beautiful plants we had brought to show them.

This little tale may help the reader to realise that there are varying grades of moss, and when purchasing care should be taken to ensure that the moss is of reasonable quality and not a bagful of old bracken and heather.

Opposite: Indoor gardens are popular presents, but they may not last without replanting. In this bowl the cyclamen would not enjoy for long the warmer conditions required by the fittonia and dracaena

Conditions for Growth

Acquiring plants and moss and arranging them in a container to provide an attractive and practical display is only the beginning; there are numerous other requirements if success is to be the reward. Besides selecting good quality plants and creating humidity, it is also necessary to provide light, airy and reasonably warm conditions. A temperature in the region of 16 to 18°C. (60 to 65°F.) is adequate for all but the more tender tropical types of plant. Excessive heat can often present more problems than temperatures that are slightly below ideal requirements, especially if the atmosphere is very dry. Excess in most things is detrimental, and it would certainly seem to apply to plants where moderation does, on the whole, give much better results.

Recently, when asked if plants would do well in a modern school, my immediate reply was 'Yes', although the school had not been visited. Modern schools provide the essential light, air and warmth, so plants should be expected to do well if the inquisitive hands of pupils are not allowed to mutilate them. The majority of plants are very much like people in their requirements – they enjoy light, a modest amount of fresh air, reasonable warmth, water and food as necessary and, above all, though it is often doubted, they do not *want* to die. Almost all the plants that succumb do so because the conditions or treatment is unsuitable, and the vast majority do so as a result of the compost becoming waterlogged from incessant watering. Some plant purchasers have the impression that the nurseryman treats his plants prior to despatch with some concoction or other to ensure that they have a limited life indoors. This is far from the truth; the supplier depends on satisfied customers whose continued custom is all important. My feeling is that attractive plants in home or office help to sell other plants to anyone who might see them, whereas dead, or dying, plants will have the opposite effect.

Another point worth bearing in mind is that when plants are sick they require to be gradually encouraged back to good health by keeping them in a warm place, watering very sparingly and temporarily discontinuing feeding. It is also important that they should not be exposed to direct sunlight. There seems to be a desire on the part of the owner to pot the ailing plant into a larger container filled with the most super of super composts. This frequently proves to be the final blow – one should pot on healthy, vigorous plants and not lame ducks. It is inevitable when repotting that the root system will suffer some damage, and this can often be the death of the sickly plant that has had its last few healthy roots destroyed in the process.

In order to succeed with indoor plants the provision of suitable growing conditions is one of the most important factors. Although the majority of plants should enjoy a light growing position only a few will tolerate full sunlight for prolonged periods. Consequently when exposed to full sunlight they will take on a hard appearance and lose much of their attraction. For most plants weak morning and evening sun is not particularly harmful, but protection is important for all but a few on the hottest days. Covering plants with a sheet of newspaper will provide a temporary answer, but it is better to remove plants to less exposed positions when the weather is very hot.

Most of the purely green plants will be better off if they are placed where light is adequate, but out of the direct rays of the sun. *Sansevieria trifasciata laurentii* is probably the best example of an indoor plant which will tolerate hot, dry conditions and seem all the better for it. Anyone who fails repeatedly with this plant has indeed got a cultural problem on their hands, and is probably misguided in being much too kind. The sansevierias in general should have much harsher treatment than the majority of plants if they are to do well, especially in respect of watering and feeding. A combination of cold and wet conditions is fatal.

Watering

If only plants could tell us exactly how much water and fertiliser they require we could all grow plants of the most superb quality. But most of our knowledge has to be gained from experience in getting to know the sort of treatment and conditions each plant requires. Unfortunately it is not the sort of knowledge that is easily passed on, as plants that would seem to be almost identical in appearance may not need the same attention. Even on the commercial nursery we are faced with the problem employee who, after many years' practical experience, still has not acquired the apparently fundamental skill of being able to water his plants properly; it can make all the difference between being a good grower and an indifferent one. In the professional side of the industry the good grower is the counterpart of the amateur whose ability with plants has won him the title of 'green fingers'.

However, having laboured the point that excessive watering is damaging for most plants some enlightenment on the correct procedure should be given. My simple rule is that the compost should be watered and allowed to dry a little before watering again. There are many excellent devices available for testing the moisture content of the compost which will give a reading indicating whether it is dry, moist or wet. Without such sophisticated equipment there is still the appendage known as a thumb with which one can test the moistness of the compost at the top of the pot. Excessively dry compost will tend to shrink away from the side of the pot and is a condition that few plants will tolerate, so care must be taken to ensure that the compost does not dry out too much between visits with the watering-can. Plants which are known to require a lot of water, such as aphelandra, *Azalea indica* and hydrangea, should be watered by plunging their pots in a bucket of water and allowing them to remain until all the air bubbles in the compost have escaped.

The majority of indoor plants require much less moisture at their roots than those last mentioned, so should be watered by filling the space between the rim of the pot and the surface of the compost. As sluggish compost is particularly unsuitable to all potted plants it is important that water should drain away fairly freely through the bottom of the pot. To encourage this with plants which have been in their pots for some time it may be necessary to use a pencil or pointed stick to break up the hard crust of soil that will have formed on the top of the pot. Need for rapid drainage is another reason for ensuring that plants do not actually stand in water, so any water that may accumulate in saucer or drip tray should be tipped away. The only exceptions to this rule would be water plants, such as cyperus, or those which require a great deal of moisture.

Where possible soft water or rain water should be used; this is particularly important in hard water areas for lime-hating plants like *Azalea indica*. Where it is impossible to provide a water butt for collecting rain water, hard tap water can be easily softened by immersing a sack of peat in a tub of water. It is, of course, important that porous sacking should be used and not a bag made of polythene.

Excessive watering will result in a very sluggish root system which will become inactive in time and result in roots rotting off; the consequence of this is eventual loss of leaves, for which all sorts of other possible causes are blamed.

Feeding your Plants

Feeding plants is also of great importance, and anyone who purchases a plant and does not buy a fertiliser of some kind at the same time cannot possibly expect the plant to do very well. Almost all the plants leaving a reputable nursery will have been fed at regular intervals. It is important that this practice should be continued indoors, but it should not be necessary for the plant to be fed quite so much, as growth in the

One plant which will tolerate hot, dry conditions well is the handsome mother-in-law's tongue, *Sansevieria trifasciata laurentii*

greenhouse is more active and requires more fertiliser in order to sustain it.

Foliage plants will benefit most from a fertiliser with a fairly high nitrogen content, while flowering plants will do very much better if the fertiliser contains a higher proportion of phosphate. A word with the supplier will quickly enlighten the purchaser as to which fertiliser should be chosen. The tendency of manufacturers of fertiliser for indoor plants is to offer products with a fairly high nitrogen content. This is understandable, as the majority of indoor plants are grown principally for their attractive foliage, and the nitrogen will certainly improve their appearance.

However, this is not necessarily a good thing for indoor flowering plants. For instance, in the past few years we have had countless questions from saintpaulia growers who say they have beautifully strong, healthy plants, but are concerned that they should produce so few flowers. It invariably transpires that they use a popular brand of high nitrogen fertiliser. The result is that the plants are producing masses of leaves

A fine specimen of *Azalea indica*. This is a lime-hating plant which should be given soft water or rain water – a point to remember in hard water areas

at the expense of flowers. The recommended action is to change the brand to a higher phosphate fertiliser, and this advice applies to almost all those who grow flower-bearing house plants.

Whatever fertiliser is used it is of the utmost importance that it should be applied to plants according to the manufacturer's directions. Don't get the idea that by doubling and trebling the recommended amounts you will do that much more good; the reverse is much more likely to be the case. Actually, it is not such a bad idea to have two different brands of fertiliser

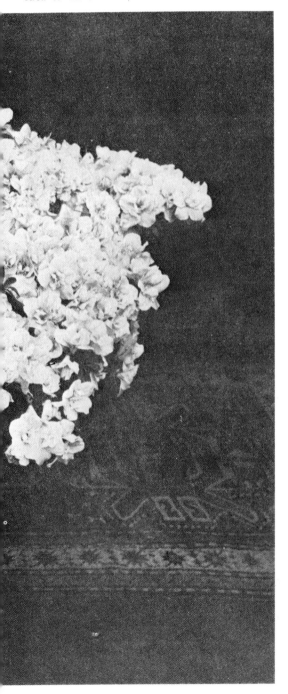

that can be applied to plants alternately. It will be no more costly over a period of time and the plants being fed will certainly appreciate the change of diet.

Spring and summer are the principal seasons for feeding plants; only those producing new growth should be fed in winter. A further precaution is to ensure that dry plants are watered before any fertiliser is applied, otherwise the roots may be damaged.

Composts and Potting

Preparing different composts for every little collection of plants would be much too tedious for the professional grower, but the amateur derives considerable pleasure from the selection, preparation and testing of various composts for his plants.

At the nursery we are often asked 'What compost do you use?' Alas, there is no simple and magical concoction that would be suitable for all the plants grown for indoor decoration today, but we do have a reasonably standard mixture for the majority of purely foliage plants. Mixing two parts John Innes Potting Compost Nos. 2 or 3 with one part sphagnum peat will produce a compost which will suit the majority of foliage plants. Or, if mixing your own J.I.P. compost, equally good results will be obtained if the quantities of peat and loam are reversed, so that the mixture contains seven parts peat and only three parts loam. The all-important factor when preparing compost for plants that will be grown entirely indoors is to ensure that the mixture is light and open. Into such a mixture the weaker plant roots that are produced indoors will penetrate much more readily.

Over the years we have seen and tried many different composts and ways of potting plants, and everyone seems to have their pet method. We are frequently told that plants should be potted into containers only one size larger than the container the plant is coming out of. This is all very well for the plant that is potted on annually, but not a lot of good for the majority of plants which require potting on only every second year. The new pot should allow about $1\frac{1}{2}$ to 2 in. of space between the pot ball and the side of the new pot and about 2 in. of space in the bottom of the pot. However, there is a danger in potting plants into containers that are too large and hopelessly out of proportion compared to the size of the plant. The majority of plants look very much better in smaller pots rather than in outsize dustbins. It is extremely difficult for small plants to root through into a large volume of compost in reasonable time, and it is important that plants become active immediately and begin filling the new compost with roots. If properly cared for in respect of feeding and watering plants will go on for many years in the same pot once they have reached the 7-in. size.

Much is also said about the need for providing free drainage in the pot by placing a layer of crocks (small pieces of broken flower pot) in the bottom of the container before introducing the compost. In the past when much heavier compost was used, often rammed hard into the pot, the use of crocks was no doubt very important. Today, however, the majority of nurseries use the lighter and more manageable plastic pots in which there is no need for crocks, as they are well supplied with drainage holes – six or more in most cases. The old clay pot had only one hole, the blockage of which could lead to stagnation of the compost and eventual root damage and loss of the plant. There is no harm in using crocks even for plastic pots, if the owner feels they are an absolute must.

For the commercial grower knowing how to pot hundreds of plants in an hour is one thing, but the majority of readers will be much more concerned with the potting of just a few plants.

Plants such as the kangaroo vine, *Cissus antarctica*, which produce long, flexible growths, are best trained on a trellis framework and pruned back to keep their shape

26

For them I have yet to find a better method than the one I have been advising for many years. This is to put an empty pot of the same size and shape as the one in which your plant is growing into the larger container with the new compost. Place sufficient compost in the bottom of the new pot to ensure that the rims of the larger pot and the 'mould' pot are level. The intervening space between large and small pot should then be filled with compost gently pressed into position with the fingers. Except for a very few plants compost should not be too firmly compacted for indoor plants.

The empty pot can now be twisted carefully and removed. Should the mould turn out to be faulty, one can replace the empty pot and push a little more compost into any gaps. The potting operation then becomes simplicity itself, as the plant is taken carefully out of its pot with the root ball intact. The best way to do this is to tap the pot sharply to loosen the compost from the edges, then, holding the stem and soil in place with one hand, turn the plant upside down so that the ball of soil slips out easily without breaking up. It can then be pressed into the perfectly shaped mould. You will have the satisfaction of knowing that the most competent expert in the land could not pot the plant any better, as it will be at exactly the right depth and the old and new compost will be in contact all the way round the pot. Better than that you just could not have!

After potting on, which is best done in April–May, the compost should be well watered from the top, giving sufficient to ensure that it is wetted right through to the bottom of the pot. Thereafter, no further water should be given for at least ten days. By keeping the compost on the dry side after potting new roots will be encouraged to spear out into the fresh compost in search of moisture, so ensuring that the plant quickly becomes re-established.

Knowing when a plant is in need of potting on is often almost impossible without removing it from its pot and checking the root development. Inspection of this kind should not be carried out too often, as unnecessary root disturbance will only damage the plant in time. House plants have an astonishing capacity for survival when growing in small pots provided feeding is not neglected, so one should not be too anxious to pot them on into ever larger containers. It is important to ensure that the root ball of the plant about to be potted is well filled with roots.

When plants are growing in pots plunged in peat troughs or beds it will often be found that roots will have penetrated through the holes in the bottom of the pot. To avoid excessive damage to the root system by cutting these away it is better to break the pot in which the plant is growing and to pot the plant with as much of the root still attached as possible.

General hardening of the foliage colour is also an indication that the plant requires additional fertiliser or potting on. It is, however, very unwise to pot on plants that are unhealthy and producing little or no new growth. Leaves turning yellow and falling off are an indication, not of need for potting, but that the plant is suffering as a result of root damage. Consequently, any attempt to pot on such a plant will only further aggravate its unhealthy condition by unnecessary root disturbance. On the other hand, with many sick plants it will often be found that the compost is at fault and rather than pot the plant into a larger container, it is better to tease away as much of the faulty compost as possible and to repot in the same or smaller container using fresh compost.

General Care

As an alternative to the relatively major operation of potting on, an inch or two of the compost from the top of the pot can be broken up with a pointed stick and removed. It can then be replaced with fresh compost in the form of a topdressing. In fact, this operation performed annually will greatly improve the performance and the appearance of one's plants. Closely matted soil on the top of the pot prevents admission of air, which in time results in tired and sour compost in which plants will do less well.

There is no particular time for giving plants an overhaul; we hear of spring cleaning, tidying up in the autumn and so forth but any time is a good time. The appearance of all plants is spoiled by the presence of dead and dying leaves, so why wait until the spring or autumn before removing them? Even in the most superb collection of plants, no matter where they have been grown or who has grown them, it is inevitable that there will at times be a percentage of dead and dying leaves. It is quite natural for older plants to shed leaves in this way as they age. Having dead leaves about is one thing, but leaving them on display for all to see is quite a different matter. A 4-ft. rubber plant is infinitely more attractive with a bare stem and half a dozen leaves at the top rather than six green leaves at the top and an equal number of droopy yellow ones lower down. So a regular rather than seasonal titivation is recommended.

Free-growing plants such as rhoicissus and *Cissus antarctica* can be pruned back to keep an attractive shape at any time. However, with such plants that produce long, flexible growth, it is often better to train the shoots onto a trellis framework of some kind. In this way the lower part of the plant from which leaves are often lost can be refurbished by winding growth back and forth down the framework rather than in the more conventional manner.

With flowering plants it is always better to remove flowers as they die in order to stop them rotting and avoid fungus troubles. With saintpaulias and cyclamen it is particularly important to ensure that when flowers are no longer attractive the complete flower stalk should be removed. Any pieces of the stem that may be left will rot back in time and damage the remainder of the plants.

The majority of glossy-leaved plants will be improved for having their leaves cleaned periodically. Most of them can be simply treated by gently wiping the leaves with a soft sponge moistened in water. Many of the glossy-leaved plants can be given a high shine by treating them with proprietary leaf-cleaning chemicals, though the gloss is often unnatural in appearance. However, care should be taken when using these products for the first time as many plants can quite easily be damaged. Kentia palms and the cast-iron plant (aspidistra) are examples of two tough plants which suffer leaf scorch and general damage when treated in this way. There is at least one of these leaf-cleaning products which is perfectly satisfactory when the temperature is reasonably high, but disastrous when the temperature drops. So it is well to be warned rather than sorry; it is sensible to test any new product on part of the plant only, allowing ten to fourteen days to elapse before deciding that no harm has been done. It is also of special importance to ensure that plants with hairy

The shining green leaves of *Asplenium nidus*, one of the most delightful house plants, have their own natural gloss and can easily be damaged by cleaning

leaves such as the saintpaulia and platycerium do not have their leaves cleaned by rubbing; a soft brush lightly used is the best way of removing dust. Although the leaves of *Asplenium nidus* are very glossy it would be ill advised to clean them in any way, except perhaps the tougher leaves on the outside of older plants.

Experimenting with new products also applies to fertiliser, compost or whatever, which should be tried out on a small scale first before being used generally. This is standard practice on the nursery and should apply equally well to plants grown at home – one cannot imagine a commercial concern indiscriminately using a new product before it has passed stringent tests on small quantities of plants.

Sailing a boat is one thing, but messing about and getting it ready for sailing is an almost equally pleasurable pastime. So, too, with plants: admiring them on display is pleasant enough, but potting, pruning and generally titivating can be just as important, and for the house plant enthusiast, just as satisfying.

And this messing about with plants seems to affect almost every section of the community. Recently an important florist customer called at the nursery to inspect our plants with two equally important customers of his own, a husband and wife who, he told us in a whispered aside, were worth a million or two. No one would have guessed it. The millionaire's entire conversation that afternoon concerned fuchsias, dracaenas and his very wonderful passion flower plant. We had the impression that he would quite happily have changed places with the man who earned his living by working with plants. The pleasure of growing and caring for plants is a pastime that knows no social boundaries.

Hairy-leaved plants, such as the saintpaulia, should never be rubbed. Cleaning should be done with a soft brush

Plants for the garden room

Garden rooms come in all shapes and sizes and are variously referred to as conservatories, sun rooms or garden rooms. Call them what you will, when heated they are mostly ideal for accommodating indoor plants of every description.

The majority of garden rooms are mass produced in the factory; others are an integral part of the house, but one cannot imagine a return to the Victorian days when many of the truly grand conservatories were constructed. The expense today would be prohibitive, and finding craftsmen to build these monster conservatories would present a considerable problem. Some years ago at Syon Park in the west of London the huge and elegant conservatory was restored to form the principal feature of a new garden centre enterprise. As an example of craftsmanship the restorers were amazed to discover that, though much of the construction was in sad need of repair, the ton-weight ventilating system at the apex of the 90-ft. high dome worked perfectly when the wire hauser control was operated.

You may visit many botanical gardens and local parks department greenhouse displays and come home filled with enthusiasm for emulating their efforts in your own garden room or greenhouse. A word of warning here: do not endeavour to copy the public authority too precisely, as many of the plants seen in their displays are totally incompatible when grouped together in a small garden room at home.

What the visitor to public authority greenhouses fails to understand is that houses open to the public are really display greenhouses. In order to support the display there are usually many greenhouses behind the scenes in which plants are grown in individual environments from where they are chosen to fill spaces in the display greenhouse as and when required. The display greenhouse will have many permanent plants, but the majority will be fly-by-nights that may be in position for only a few days before being replaced.

It really is not practicable to grow a range of plants with differing temperature, humidity and light requirements together under the same roof and expect them all to do well. Frequently I am invited to inspect the plant collections of acquaintances and give my opinion as to why a certain plant does not do so well. More often than not the garden room enthusiast is paying the price of trying to emulate the example of the botanic garden display and meeting with the customary failure. It is no good trying to grow successfully in the same conditions such incompatible subjects as cyclamen and crotons, for example. The former prefers cool, light

conditions, while the latter must have a temperature in the region of 18°C. (65°F.) if it is to do anything at all. It would be even more of a problem to attempt to grow cyclamen with members of the *Marantaceae* or philodendron family which must have the higher temperature and heavy shade in addition. Both would be totally unsuited to accompany the light- and cool-loving cyclamen.

So the first lesson is to be selective and choose the sort of plants that are likely to do well together. The A to Z chapter will indicate the light, temperature and general conditions suited to particular plants.

Construction of the garden room is very much a question of the space available and what one can afford to pay. Rooms can either be isolated in the garden in the same way as a greenhouse, or they may be attached to the house. An extension to the house is more satisfactory in many ways, as it will be cheaper to heat and less costly to construct. The wall of the house forms one wall of the garden room, keeping it very much warmer; the position will also be less exposed to the elements. In turn the garden room will add a pleasant dimension to the room leading into it, so there are benefits all round. Besides these advantages plants can be seen and enjoyed if they are close at hand, and they can be looked after with less inconvenience.

Another very important consideration when planning the garden room is to ensure that there is adequate ventilation. As with a small greenhouse, the first thought will be to make sure that there is proper insulation to keep heating costs as low as possible. This is understandable when it is realised just how costly it can be to heat a reasonably sized garden room over the course of the year. However, ventilation is an equally important consideration for the summer months. All windows and the door will frequently have to be opened in order to reduce the temperature in the room.

On cooler days it is an advantage if the door is on the more sheltered side of the room. Opening the door on the northerly, or exposed, side can create havoc in cold and windy weather. The area of the garden room is very often dictated by limitations of the site, or one's purse, but where possible provision should be made for reasonable head room, as many of the plants used to create a display will be of climbing habit and will need 8 to 10 ft. of floor to ceiling height in which to develop. This will suit the majority of plants that one is likely to use. Grand though it may seem to have exotic plants and flowers cascading down from supports and columns, pests will often go unnoticed when at a height until it is too late for insecticides to be really effective, especially with plants such as the stephanotis and hoya types. Their twisting stems provide an excellent breeding ground for mealy bug which can be so destructive, unsightly and difficult to control once it has taken a firm hold.

Seldom can we stress too fully the need for providing adequate light in order to grow plants successfully. But protection from direct sunlight is equally important, so provision must be made for shielding plants from the strong, direct rays of the sun. The baking oven effect created by clear glass in a small room on a hot summer's day can spell death to the majority of all but the most durable plants. A variety of measures can be employed to protect plants from the sun, but most of them are either messy or unattractive. Coating the glass with distemper or whitewash is cheap and effective but messy, and using roller blinds is effective, cumbersome and very expensive in most cases. Flat sheets of white polystyrene clipped to the inside of the glass bars is far and away the best method to my mind, though it must be remembered that this is an inflammable material. However, these sheets are inexpensive, efficient and not unattractive. Besides these qualities they can be easily removed, which is an important factor during the winter months when plants require all the light available. Furthermore, against the white background plants are set off much more attractively, particularly those with green foliage.

Surprisingly, a new greenhouse, or garden room for that matter, is not necessarily the best place in which to grow the more difficult plants. The old hands in the nursery business invariably show some reluctance when asked to care for new greenhouses on a new site – they feel that much better crops are produced once the greenhouse has been producing plants for a year or two.

The foregoing is mentioned so that the enthusiast with the new garden room does not stock up his new plaything with the most difficult and exotic plants that the nurseryman can supply. Although the initial display might not be so startlingly effective, use of less delicate plants in the first twelve months or so will prove to be much more satisfactory in the end. Incidentally, for the beginner it is infinitely more satisfying to select and grow easy plants well at the outset, rather than be disappointed by the sight of difficult plants deteriorating.

Here again, when stocking a new plant room it would be wise to seek the advice of the plant supplier who will be able to recommend the subjects likely to do best in the prevailing conditions. If the supplier is wise he will not take advantage of the purchaser's ignorance; it will be to his advantage if plants succeed – any that fail he may well have to replace.

When equipping the garden room the main consideration should be given to the plants rather than to the owner, who may use it as a refuge from the general cares of daily life. Carpeted floors would add that touch of luxury, but one feels that more consideration would be given to the carpet rather than the plants. A tiled, stone, or similar material impervious to moisture would be much more suitable when watering and generally caring for plants in the conservatory. Too much emphasis cannot be placed on the need for damping the floor at the same time when watering plants in the garden room or conservatory. On warm days damping of this kind should be repeated several times in order to maintain the correct humidity level, but in most instances the plant pots will only need watering at most once each day, bearing in mind that there are exceptions such as the hydrangea. It is also worth bearing in mind that in hot, dry conditions pests, such as red spider mites, multiply much more rapidly.

There is no lack of choice when it comes to selecting suitable means of heating the garden room. This can quite often be incorporated with the central heating of the house. Cost and suitability is again the major consideration, but whatever method is used it must be adequate for the colder nights of the year; this may entail budgeting for a little more heat than is likely to be needed. It is pointless to have adequate heating for 364 days of the year if on the 365th it should prove to be insufficient – one really cold night can put paid to an entire collection of plants.

Advice on fitting out the interior can only be general as everyone's taste will differ and arranging plants and interior décor is very much a personal matter. Whether plants are made permanent features by planting them in beds of compost on the floor, or portable by growing them in pots on raised staging, are also matters for individual taste.

Both these methods have their merits. Planted directly into beds of prepared compost, or with plant pots plunged to their rims in moist peat, plants will usually grow very much more vigorously. However, left in their pots and placed on staging at waist level one can have the pleasure of rearranging plants, or using them for decoration in other parts of the house whenever required. Handling plants, titivating, cleaning, feeding and such like is all part of the relaxing pleasure that plants bring to many of us, so one should think twice before planting them out in more permanent positions.

33

Personally, I am a great believer in picking plants up regularly and removing the odd dead leaves or algae from the top of the compost before replacing them on the table or staging. It gives plants a much fresher appearance and by handling them in this way we are able to see immediately if there are any pests or disease present. Getting into the habit of picking plants up and tidying them over is an operation that many plant retailers could well adopt to their advantage. The sight of tired, uncared-for plants which have obviously been left un-attended for weeks on end in the shop or garden centre often makes me wonder just how many more plants the retailer could sell if he presented them better, and was a trifle more considerate about their general well-being.

Earlier in this chapter mention was made of the unique Syon Park conservatory which was the principal attraction of a new garden centre project. We were invited to plant the central section of the conservatory with indoor plants; the temperature to be maintained at a constant minimum in the region of 13°C. (60°F.). The floor was completely flagged over with natural paving stone and there was ample head room for any plants from the nursery that we cared to bring along.

Bearing in mind the expected flow of visitors reasonably wide pathways were considered essential. It was decided that the planting should be at floor level and that large beds for planting should be contained by low walls about 1 ft. in height. Beds were filled with sphagnum peat to just below the height of the surrounding wall. Into these beds a wide selection of plants were plunged as deeply as the peat would allow – some of the larger pots were only half buried.

On the sunny south side larger plants were used so that they would provide shade for other plants. These larger plants were mainly forms of ficus which developed a number of brown leaves at the beginning, but soon adapted them-selves to the rather hot position. In a matter of two years they went berserk and had to be drastically pruned back to more manageable proportions. One reason for the abundant growth was that roots had penetrated to the beds of peat, either through the bottom of the pot, or in some instances over the top. The free root-run and regular feed directed into the pots helped maintain active growth and colour.

Of the plants installed the philodendrons, ficus and scheffleras proved to be the most satisfactory. Stephanotis happily made its way to the top of high pillars and produced long strands of growth that flowered with reasonable freedom, but could not be fully appreciated from the floor below. Flower scent was missed,

Opposite: The modern sun or garden room provides a pleasant link between garden and house. A floor covering impervious to moisture is desirable

35

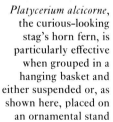

36

and this, after all, is one of the major attractions of *Stephanotis floribunda*. A plant of *Passiflora caerulea* on an adjacent pillar also got somewhat out of hand – not unusual with this free-growing plant which, consequently, is not particularly suited to smaller garden rooms.

Ficus benghalensis proved to be the most rampant grower of all, developing into a considerable tree with many strong branches at all levels in less than three years. Fortunately it does not take unkindly to annual, almost savage pruning. If you have the space and a really dominant plant is required, then this could well be the one.

For lower positions where a bold effect was required we used some of the philodendrons with radiating leaves. In particular *P. bipinnatifidum* did a grand job by filling in large areas

with their large, glossy, and serrated leaves. Being an aroid, masses of roots were produced along the main stem which in time found their way into the peat beds, and from then on there was no stopping them.

Of all the plants in this conservatory the most popular and interesting to visitors has been the stag's horn fern, *Platycerium alcicorne*, despite the fact that all sorts of other exotic plants have been on display; crotons, anthuriums, citrus and the like. This is frequently the case: the plant with interesting and unusual foliage will often have more appeal than the colourful or floriferous subject.

Actually, any plant that can be grown in a hanging basket, or on a piece of bark in the case of the stag's horn fern, and suspended from the ceiling gives the garden room another dimension.

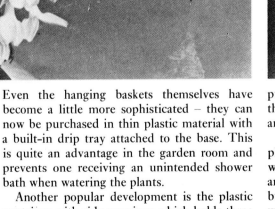

Even the hanging baskets themselves have become a little more sophisticated – they can now be purchased in thin plastic material with a built-in drip tray attached to the base. This is quite an advantage in the garden room and prevents one receiving an unintended shower bath when watering the plants.

Another popular development is the plastic container with side openings which holds three small plants and comes in a variety of colours. Plants in these drip-free containers can be used equally well indoors and suspended near a window. It will be important to ensure that the compost does not become saturated as these containers do not have any form of drainage holes through which excess water can escape. When planting it should be borne in mind that a better effect can sometimes be achieved by putting three plants of the same variety in these three-in-one containers rather than a mixed arrangement.

In the garden room a wide assortment of house plants can also be grown in pots suspended in wall brackets. In the living-room wall brackets are only suitable for the hardier types of plant, but the moister conditions in the garden room will allow for the use of many more delicate plants. Columneas are excellent for both hanging baskets and wall brackets, and the delightful *Campanula isophylla*, the star of Bethlehem, is an essential plant where cooler conditions prevail.

For continuity of colour throughout late spring, summer and early autumn there surely cannot be any plant that compares with the fuchsia. Indoors the indifferent amount of light

Campanula isophylla, a delightful trailing plant for a hanging basket

37

Top: Prolific and colourful, fuchsias are especially effective in a hanging basket. This is the white variety Evensong

Bottom: Because of its free-growing habit, *Passiflora caerulea*, the passion flower, is suitable only for the larger garden room

Opposite: A corner of a garden room. Displayed here, from left to right, are a codiaeum, *Campanula isophylla, Dracaena deremensis rhoersii, Episcia cupreata, Dracaena marginata concinna, Scindapsus aureus* Marble Queen, *Cussonia spicata* and, in the foreground, a gloxinia

inevitably results in premature loss of flowers and buds, but it is quite the most prolific flowering plant in the greenhouse or garden room. Growing advice amounts to little more than keeping the plants in reasonably good light – not full sun under glass – watering and feeding regularly and potting on into reasonably large containers fairly early in the season. Try putting five or six cuttings in a large basket early in the season, mid-April say, and you will be quite amazed by the display provided with very little effort on your part only a few months later. For basket work choose varieties that the nurseryman lists as being suitable for that purpose. There are so many to choose from it would be impossible to list them here. Visit any retail nursery in the spring and make your choice – they will be available in all colours and sizes from standards down to little more than rooted cuttings. Remember the earlier advice: ask the man in charge and he will recommend the most suitable plants for the purpose you have in mind.

Besides the smaller and hanging plants a few climbers should be considered for the garden room, but this should be done carefully as the majority grow rapidly in good conditions. With the small greenhouse or garden room there is always the temptation at the beginning to fill the available space with plants as quickly as possible. The seemingly vast open space may appear a trifle daunting at the outset, and getting sufficient plants to fill the garden room may seem a quite hopeless task. But, mark my words, this is a wholly unjustified concern.

In any neighbourhood there are countless greenhouses and garden rooms choc-a-bloc with plants of every description; many of them over-grown, pest ridden and past their best. You can rest assured that once the various house plant owners get to know of your new acquisition they will not be slow to offer the odd gift to set up your collection of plants. This may appear very matey and friendly, but it does have its drawbacks. You invariably feel indebted to the donor and, worse still, once you have accepted the bug-ridden chlorophytum, or what-ever, you are obliged to keep it for fear of causing offence when the previous owner pays you a visit and finds his 'gift' missing from the collection!

Worst of all, you have got off to a very bad start in that you may have introduced a ready-made collection of pests that will make every effort to develop and multiply and get onto all the other plants you will subsequently acquire. So, at the start, be selective – accept the odd useful plant gift, but avoid a headlong rush to take all that is offered. Let there be no

A fine specimen of codiaeum. Any plant collection is enhanced by the codiaeums with their wide variations of leaf colour in yellows, greens and reds

Bottom: Good plants need sufficient space between them to allow in light and air but should not be arranged in isolation

mistake, the garden room will be filled to capacity in a remarkably short space of time. It won't take many weeks before you will be standing with a pot of plants in each hand wondering where in the world you are going to put them.

This situation invariably leads to crowding of plants, the consequence being that all of them do less well. The alternative is simply a choice between quality and quantity – good plants need adequate space in which to grow, and given reasonable space plants look so much better. This entails leaving a little air space between each plant when setting them out on the staging, but does not imply that they ought to be set miles apart in splendid isolation. Far from it; almost all plants seem to do better when growing in the proximity of others. Young plants can, of course, be left fairly close together until they begin to develop more mature leaves.

If the garden room is attached to the house, then the house wall should be brought into use as a support for climbing plants. All sorts of fittings are available but I am still a great believer in the old-fashioned trellis as a means of support. The timber will be greatly improved by a couple of coats of white paint, which will set off the plants well. As an alternative to the conventional diamond-shaped trellis try making your own up in a squared rather than a diamond pattern.

A little space should be allowed for between the trellis and the wall so that plants can be easily tied and to allow for circulation of air. Constructed in light timber, trellis of this kind can also be used for camouflaging unsightly central supports in the larger plant room. Here again one may have climbing plants by preparing a bed of compost at the foot of the post, or by having plants in free-standing decorative containers.

Attractive, unfussy plant containers can make all the difference to the elegant appearance of the room. It is preferable to have a few expensive containers filled with well-chosen plants rather than a motley collection of cheaper plant containers of all shapes and sizes. Mobile containers, mounted if necessary on castors, will give much more pleasure than plants embedded in mounds of peat or compost, especially to the lady of the house who can exercise that peculiarly feminine trait of moving around the furniture and plants at regular intervals! As mentioned earlier, this is not such a problem where plants are concerned provided there is no radical change in the temperature or light availability in the new position.

For a really spick-and-span garden room the possibility of having a small support green-

Plant cases in which accurate control of temperature and humidity can be maintained may appeal to the specialist collector. This case contains an impressive display of saintpaulias

house is worth considering – similar to the botanic garden principle mentioned earlier. If the sundry operations required to keep a collection of plants in good condition are all performed in the garden room it soon becomes cluttered with all sorts of odds and ends for potting, propagating and such like. It is much better to have a special place like the small greenhouse for these tasks. It will also be invaluable as a sick bay where plants may be put to recover (or die peacefully!) instead of being left in the plant room to mar its appearance.

Besides the plant room attached to the outside of the house there is also the possibility of adapting a spare room indoors for this purpose. There are elaborate plant cases on the market specifically intended for accommodating indoor plants, many of them quite sophisticated, having light, temperature, and even humidity controls built in. Adjustable shelves make it possible for a wide range of smaller plants to be grown very successfully. Under such carefully controlled conditions the saintpaulia does particularly well, and could well provide a specialist interest for the real enthusiast.

Almost all the plants included in the A to Z chapter would be suitable for the garden room provided the temperature matches that suggested for the particular plants. Grapes are not included in the A to Z, but having a vine in the plant room is quite a possibility and will provide cool shade for other plants besides a crop of grapes. The best way to treat vines in a small room of the sort we have in mind is to plant them outside the building and to train the stem of the plant through a hole in the wall. Trained to wires suspended from the ceiling of the garden room they

will be quite effective and are very easy to care for. Once established, vines will make rapid growth and will require periodic trimming back during the growing season. In winter they should be cut back to two eyes from the main stem.

We seldom think of garden conservatories without recalling the experience of a florist who was commissioned to plant up and maintain a rather grand Victorian-style conservatory in the home counties. Many mature plants were installed and doing very well until a collection of tropical birds was introduced. One rather ferocious parrot had a habit of pecking through the stems of some of the more mature plants, and seemed to have a particular partiality for *Aralia elegantissima*. So much so that the contract man in charge of maintenance stood there one day and watched as the tall stem of one of these plants toppled and fell to the floor, Polly having performed a very creditable bit of tree felling.

Nothing was safe – other parrots in the collection were felled by Polly's flashing beak, never to move again. Hearing accounts of these events from the contractor were amusing enough, but it became positively hilarious when the antics of his girl in charge of watering the plants were related. It seems that her equipment consisted of a watering-can in one hand, a crash helmet on her head and a stout stick in the other hand with which to discourage the deadly dive bombing attacks of Polly!

We all have our problems when it comes to plant care indoors, but in future when your rubber plant decides to shed a leaf it may be some consolation to remember our crash-helmeted plant girl and the perils of Polly.

41

Specimen plants for special positions

Sometimes a plant is required for a special display point, a corner of a hall or living room which demands one dominant feature. For these positions one thinks of more majestic plants with architectural shapes to their leaves, or plants of striking appearance – the sort of plant which does not need the support of other plants around it in order to create a pleasing effect. Unfortunately there are all too few of these specimen plants available today. And to see them in their full glory they must be of specimen size when purchased, as many do not produce fully mature leaves until they are several years old.

Almost all of them are purely green foliage plants, so are ideally suitable for the lighter colours used in modern decor. In no particular

order, but with a possible bias towards my own favourites, the following are suggested for that very special position where ample space is available to show the plant off to best advantage, not forgetting headroom.

Schefflera

When well grown there can be few more elegant specimen plants. Green, seven- to nine-fingered leaves are carried on 2-ft. long petioles attached to a stout central stem. When confined to large pots they will attain a height of some 20 ft. in time. Being symmetrical plants, they may well form a central feature in a room or office, as they are equally attractive from all view points. Care is needed when handling the plants as there is no way of replacing leaves that may be inadver-

tently knocked off. In reasonable conditions the schefflera is not in the least difficult to care for.

Pandanus

Some of the majestic screw pines have beautiful saw-edged yellow leaves and may attain a height of 8 to 12 ft. when roots are confined to a plant pot, or large tub. Tightly overlapping leaves radiate in all directions and may give the really super plant a diameter in the region of 12 ft. Light, warm conditions are needed and, because of the saw-edged leaves, a position away from the general stream of humanity that may be passing. Alas, plants are in acutely short supply and take many, many years to reach maturity, so it may be a little unfair even to mention the superb pandanus as a worthwhile specimen plant.

Opposite:
The symmetrical foliage of *Schefflera actinophylla* can be viewed equally well from any side, a valuable attribute for a specimen plant

The pandanus, or screw pine, requires plenty of room for its graceful, overlapping leaves

Tolerating a wide
range of conditions,
*Monstera pertusa
borsigiana* is an
excellent specimen
plant with its huge,
deeply serrated leaves

Monstera

Known to everyone, the monsteras have stood the test of time and are still very much in demand as individual specimen plants. Close inspection of really mature monstera leaves suggests that Mother Nature was in particularly good form when she created them. Deeply serrated along both sides, mature leaves are also perforated – perforations which begin at the midrib and gradually reduce in size as they fan out from the centre of the leaf. These are grand plants to have and not difficult to manage in warm, moist and shaded conditions. They do infinitely better if the aerial roots are allowed a free run in a bed of peat – standing plants in a large container filled with peat can make this possible.

Dracaena marginata

Green leaves edged with a thin strip of red are narrow and pointed, and give this plant a stark, elegant appearance, seen to best effect when several plants of varying height are grouped together in a container. Light, fairly dry conditions are best, also moderate watering. Like most dracaenas, these plants lose their lower leaves as the plant extends in height, but attractive silver-coloured stems make the loss of leaves much easier to bear.

Ficus benjamina

The weeping fig has small, oval-shaped, glossy green leaves and may grow to a height of 20 ft. in a large pot. Conditions similar to those suggested for the monstera are best. These plants dislike being moved from place to place, so should be left alone when obviously settled and growing well.

Ficus lyrata

The glossy green leaves of this plant are shaped like the body of a violin and have faint yellow veins running through them, but the overall impression is purely green. Not particularly easy to care for, it does better if the roots are allowed to grow through the bottom of the pot and into a container filled with moist peat. It takes many years to reach maturity but a height of 20 ft. is quite possible when plants are growing in large pots. However, by the time plants attain this height they will have almost inevitably lost most of their lower leaves. Conditions required are warm, moist and shaded; the temperature should not fall below 16°C. (60°F.).

Philodendron bipinnatifidum

Among the lower growing plants with spreading leaves this one has few rivals where bolder specimens are required. Large, deeply serrated leaves radiate from a stout central stem and

are a dark, glossy green in colour. Excellent plants for situations by a large pool, particularly if it is possible to allow the aerial roots into the water. In this way the plant can draw up all the moisture required and there should be much less need to water the actual compost in which the plant is growing. It is easy to care for if treated in the same way as the monstera.

Ficus benghalensis

The natural downy covering on the leaves of this plant prevent it becoming as popular as it might be; glossy leaves seem to be an important requirement of foliage plants indoors. Where space is adequate and conditions reasonable growth can be quite spectacular, so it is a useful plant if only for this reason. Plants take on tree proportions with many branches when fully developed, and a height of some 30 ft. in dustbin-sized containers is quite possible.

Many other philodendrons and ficuses could be added to the list of plants which will attain specimen size when well grown, but many of them are difficult to obtain. However, it can be generally assumed that any plant with large leaves can be grown into mature specimens if time and conditions are available. *Philodendron hastatum*, *tuxla*, Burgundy and *lacineatum* are examples. Hederas, rhoicissus and such like may also be grown to considerable size, but they lack the majestic appearance of the plants that have been listed here.

Plants for office display

However impersonal the vast concrete and glass tower block office may be in other respects, in most cases they provide reasonable conditions in which to grow decorative plants. And there is no doubt that the interior of all such offices have their appearance greatly improved and softened by the introduction of growing plants.

It will cost practically nothing for the typist to purchase a tradescantia in a pot to decorate the nearest window-sill, but it may involve the owner in a considerable outlay if the entire office area is to be landscaped with indoor plants. The window-sill plant is usually the property and responsibility of the person working in the vicinity and need not involve any expense. But if a plant collection is to be kept, it should be looked after and removed when, as so often happens, the plants have died and the collection becomes little more than one of flower pots with dry, baked compost and no plants in sight. The dry conditions created by the often too-high temperatures of the modern office is the principal reason for plants deteriorating. Exposure to excessive sunlight through unprotected glass can also be harmful to many of the shade-loving plants.

When selecting plants for offices it is particularly important to ensure that they will at least be reasonably suitable for the conditions that prevail. Although light is important, exposure to full sunlight on the south side of the building would quickly prove fatal to the majority of indoor plants. For exposed sunny positions only the really tough sansevieria type of plant is suitable. For the hot office it would also be unwise to select plants which prefer cooler conditions. In particular the ivies and *Cissus antarctica* would not be expected to survive for more than a few weeks in really hot, arid situations. The A to Z chapter indicates the sort of conditions that particular plants are likely to enjoy, so there is no need to provide a duplicate list here.

To impress visitors it is important to provide a display of plants in the office or hotel reception area. In recent years it has been proved, however, that it is equally important to provide amenable conditions where the actual work is taking place – in the offices themselves.

Consequently, a small revolution has taken place since office landscaping (*bureaulandschaft*) came into being in Germany. An incredible number of plants are required annually, both for new schemes and to titivate existing ones. Landscaping of this kind has resulted in an entirely new concept in utilising available office floor space. No longer is it necessary to have a multitude of small offices segregated from one another by interior walls. Open-plan layouts

Opposite: *Anthurium scherzerianum*, the variegated form of *Aralia sieboldii* (syn. *Fatsia japonica*), and *Araucaria excelsa*, the Norfolk Island pine

have become the fashion with filing cabinets, screens and foliage plants used to form divisions between departments, or individual areas. One of the many advantages of these schemes is the flexibility they permit – it is no longer necessary to demolish walls to increase or reduce the size of particular departments; the screens and potted plants can simply be moved one way or the other in order to make the alterations.

The importance of landscaping office interiors with plants has gone some way beyond sending the junior to the nearest flower shop to purchase a rubber plant. Today there are specialists in the field who make the installation and maintenance of foliage plants in offices a full-time occupation. They will estimate the cost of the proposed landscaping, and will then be able to supply containers, compost and plants when required. A complete maintenance service for watering, feeding, cleaning and plant replacement can also be contracted for.

To reduce the cost of maintaining plants the office landscaper has developed much more sophisticated plant containers than we would

Many house plants adapt easily to the light, airy conditions of a modern office

have imagined possible only a few years ago. Better design has given these containers much more eye appeal, but the really important step has been made in providing some of them with artificial bottoms.

The artificial bottom allows for a reservoir of water that can be gradually drawn upon by the compost as it dries out. There are many variations, but the general principle is that a piece of plastic pipe leads from just above the surface of the compost into the reservoir, which can be topped up as necessary. Nylon wicks about 2 in. in width and 8 in. long are laid flat in the bottom of the container with one end in the water prior to the introduction of compost. The number of wicks will vary according to the size of the container – generally three or four are required for a container 2 ft. in diameter. A dipstick through the plastic supply pipe can be used to check when the water requires topping up. Water is then drawn by capillary action from the reservoir into the compost as required and, although not one hundred per cent. accurate, it does ensure that the compost is being regularly watered.

It goes without saying that this is a most essential requirement in the hot, dry atmosphere of an office. It is also a very much better system than having the more conventional and simple containers for, at the hands of the inexperienced person, at home or in the office, plants seldom do as well as they might, as they are either parched from inadequate dribbles of water, or completely saturated from regular flooding of the compost.

For the plant maintenance man the advantage of all this is very obvious – instead of his staff paying twice-weekly visits to the many offices on his round they can reduce the frequency to about once each fortnight. On these visits the water level is topped up, the compost is fed and general maintenance and necessary plant replacements are seen to.

When drawing up contracts for office landscaping schemes of this kind the office chief should come to a clear understanding concerning plants that are likely to fail, so that they can be replaced without difficulty. No matter how wonderful the environment, maintenance and general conditions may be, it is almost inevitable that some plants will succumb.

Besides offices there are hotels, schools and such places as shopping precincts where plants are considered to be an essential part of the environment. Many years ago a request for the nursery to provide a planting scheme for a shopping centre in the north of England was met very much with tongue in cheek, as it was one of our first experiences of such a venture.

The invaluable rubber plant, *Ficus elastica robusta*, is an ideal choice for the formal setting of an office or reception hall

49

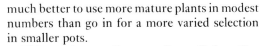

Opposite: Neoregelia carolinae tricolor (left foreground), the tall *Ficus elastica schryvereana, Cissus antarctica* and *Tradescantia bicolor*

Plants are used increasingly for landscaping effect in reception areas and offices. This collection includes a dieffenbachia, *Ficus elastica robusta, Hedera canariensis*, peperomia and tradescantia

Plants were required for raised beds in the pedestrian way of the L-shaped building. Temperature was to be maintained at not less than 16°C. (60°F.) and the principal source of light was to be from large, reinforced glass side windows. Plants were to be free planted in J.I.P.3 compost with good drainage provided.

Visiting the centre many years later it was particularly pleasing to see that my tongue-in-cheek suggestions for planting had been carried out and that the plants were doing particularly well – this in spite of a continual flow of shoppers. Beds were raised about 5 ft. from the floor with bench seating for shoppers at the base of each container. Being at higher level seemed to protect the plants from the inquisitive fingers of passers-by, which is a considerable advantage in itself.

In any scheme of this kind it is essential that only the more durable of indoor plants be used, and those with large, distinctive leaves are particularly suitable; monsteras, schefflera and *Philodendron bipinnatifidum* being good examples. Where space is adequate it is very

much better to use more mature plants in modest numbers than go in for a more varied selection in smaller pots.

This advice applies equally well in office planting schemes; it is much more impressive and less troublesome to have a smaller number of mature plants that will settle down more readily and be much less bother when it comes to maintenance. Inspection of any office landscaping layout will show that by far the most fatalities are among the smaller plants.

The reception area office display is frequently the most impressive, so invariably the most costly to install. In these areas there is scope for the landscaper to provide an impressive display, and it is an advantage if water, moving or still, can be incorporated. If nothing else it will provide an agreeably moist atmosphere around plants, which can only be advantageous. Also, any form of movement in a display will attract the eye; it need only be a drip of water from a concealed header tank. And once the casual eye has been attracted it will begin to see the beauty of flowers and plants around the pool, which might have otherwise gone more or less unnoticed. By suggesting water movement around plants as an additional attraction in a display one does not necessarily have a Niagara in mind.

When discussing the supply of plants for office schemes advice should be sought from the landscaper who will have practical experience of what will do well (and where it will do well) and what will not. Exotic and colourful though they may be, containers filled with flamboyant crotons and other delicate tropical plants are not especially practical. And the landscaper who may be persuaded to include above-average quantities of delicate plants would be wise to exclude these from his plant replacement agreement.

Yet, it is surprising the number of plants that do perfectly well in modern offices today which only a few short years ago were looked upon very much as delicate subjects. One of the best examples may be found among the dieffenbachias, the majority of which the gardening books still lump together as being stove (very hot greenhouse) plants of notoriously delicate nature. However, in many planting schemes these will be found to be outliving plants that are usually considered much more durable.

When considering plants as a landscaping feature in the office it should be remembered that they are a feature and should be used as such by giving them a prominent position. Avoid the temptation to use plants for covering up unsightly features as this is not their function, and they seldom do well when tucked away in corners, however well they may be cared for.

New plants from old

This is where our green-fingered friends seem to come into their own – others can grow bigger and more beautiful plants, and get their African violets to flower regularly each year, but the friend who produces new plants from bits and pieces of cuttings does seem to have that extra bit of magic at his fingertips. But it really only requires a few simple rules in order to become surprisingly successful. Luck plays a very small part; it is the material and conditions which make all the difference between success and failure.

For the most part cuttings of indoor plants are not too difficult to propagate, particularly if reasonable facilities are provided for housing them.

Although it may seem pointless to describe in detail the function of the propagating department of a major nursery where literally millions of house plant cuttings are rooted annually, a brief look at some of the methods employed may be of some benefit. Once the novice appreciates the principles involved he is half way towards success.

Firstly, the nurseryman requires heated greenhouse space – large or small depending on his needs – the temperature to be maintained in the region of 18 to 21°C. (65 to 70°F.). For best results enclosed propagating beds are necessary, with heating pipes in the lower part of the enclosed area. Over the heating pipes a variety of materials may be used for supporting the cutting bed, which is usually prepared from sphagnum peat by itself, or with a small quantity of sharp sand added.

The supporting material is usually stiff metal mesh covered with perforated polythene which allows heat from the pipes to flow freely upwards through the propagating medium. This ensures that the bed is maintained at the comparatively high temperature level essential to good results.

Cuttings inserted into such a peat bed (4 to 6 in. in depth) will quickly show their appreciation and produce roots in the minimum length of time. The nurseryman is further aided in his efforts by a little light shade on the greenhouse and mist spray lines suspended over the cutting beds. The spray lines are all important, as they can be regulated to come into operation at set times, frequency depending on the prevailing weather conditions. When very hot it would be essential that the mist unit is activated at frequent intervals during the course of the day. The regular fine spray ensures that neither cuttings nor propagating bed is allowed to dry out, which would in most instances result in failure.

Hygiene is a further essential requirement, so the propagating beds must be steam sterilised after each batch of cuttings has gone through.

Neglect to do so would mean that fungus spores remain active in the beds and attack any cuttings that are subsequently inserted. Fresh or sterilised peat should be used with each new batch of cutting material. For the house plant grower propagating only a few plants at home it would be wise to use fresh peat each time. Even on the nursery the medium in which cuttings have been rooted is renewed after every second or third lot of cuttings has gone through, or sooner if there is a high percentage of failure.

Having taken every precaution with sterilised propagating beds, adequate heat, moisture and such like, it can all be to no avail if the cuttings or the plants from which the cuttings have been removed are sub-standard. Consequently, on the nursery, if there is the slightest doubt concerning the suitability of cutting material it is discarded. Any faulty cuttings that find their way into the propagating beds will quickly rot and die, with the result that healthy cuttings surrounding them are in time affected.

For the average house plant grower with an indifferent collection of plants who wishes to experiment with the mysteries of propagation the chances of success are reduced from the outset. One would not wish to damn his chances too firmly, but the point is made simply to emphasise that the novice must be prepared to sacrifice some of the better material on his plants from which to take cuttings if he wishes to succeed. The poor, weedy bits that can be more easily spared seldom do well, even though other conditions such as temperature may be ideal.

Frequently we hear that some particular exercise or other is child's play, and this is certainly so when propagating some of the easier indoor plants. And there is no better way of encouraging youngsters to take an interest in plants than to get them to propagate some of the simpler cuttings for themselves. My own young daughter did just this with a few cuttings of Christmas cactus (*Schlumbergera buckleyi*) some years ago and it is now one of our most treasured possessions, cared for by the young lady in question who never fails to inform visitors that it is *her* plant.

Perhaps we should first consider the various methods of propagation and the different types of plants that can be increased by their use.

Seed

For the beginner wishing to build up a collection of plants rapidly the most satisfactory method is to raise them from seed, though this may be a somewhat slow process with many of them. The main advantage is that it is not necessary to have a collection of plants or a donation of cuttings before you start, as seed can be easily purchased, preferably from a supplier who

Schlumbergera buckleyi, the showy Christmas cactus, is easily propagated from cuttings

specialises in the unusual. The seed supplier will almost invariably provide advice on the general conditions needed in order to get the best results.

Shallow containers, seed boxes or seed pans should be used for sowing, and John Innes No. 1 compost will be ideal for the purpose. Sow in moist compost and keep in a lightly shaded place to begin with; covering the container with a sheet of glass when the seeds are sown will encourage germination. When the seedlings are large enough to handle they should be transferred to J.I.P.2 compost, or similar, and at this time can either be spaced out in the seed boxes again for a spell or put individually into small pots.

Once the seedlings are established in small pots it is a good time for indulging in a bit of barter with any acquaintance who may have a collection of plants. Whether you are able to arrange an exchange or not it will be advisable to dispose of the majority of young plants if the germination has been satisfactory, as it will be impossible to grow them all on to maturity in a

limited space. Only the best seedlings should be saved for your own use.

Runners and Offsets

There are many plants that one can use to encourage the young propagator, and the best is probably the chlorophytum or spider plant. If a larger plant with young plants attached is placed in the centre of a tray or seed box filled with J.I.P.2 compost the young plantlets can be pegged down all around the pot in the same way as strawberry runners, and they will root in little time without much bother. When obviously growing on their own roots they can be snipped away from the parent plant and potted up individually, to begin with in small pots of the same compost.

In any event, in order to have fresh, healthy plants it is advisable to propagate chlorophytum plants in this way every second or third year. When young plants have rooted they should replace the tired, older plants which can either be disposed of or passed on to someone else to care for!

Other plants in the very-easy-to-propagate range that can be treated in a similar fashion are the pick-a-back plant (*Tolmiea menziesii*) and *Saxifraga sarmentosa*. The latter is given the common name of mother-of-thousands on account of the masses of young plantlets that hang permanently from the parent, making it an interesting rather than an attractive plant.

Bromeliads are best increased by means of seed if quantities are wanted, but for modest requirements the best method is to remove and pot up individually the small offsets that develop around the base of older plants, particularly after they have produced flowers. Avoid removing them too soon; allow a few leaves to develop on each young plant before cutting it away with a sharp knife and potting up individually, in peat to begin with.

The pineapple is the only edible bromeliad and the only member of this fascinating family that is a commercial proposition in anything other than a decorative sense. Another interesting aspect of the pineapple is that new plants can (if one is lucky) be propagated by removing the tufted top of the fruit and allowing it to dry a little before pressing it into a shallow bed of sand under which there is a peaty compost. In good heat roots will more easily form in the sand before finding their way into the compost beneath. The more decorative variegated pineapple produces colourful, barely edible fruits when about four years old. When fully ripe, young plantlets form around the top of the fruit. These would seem ideal for propagating new plants, but my experience suggests that such

pieces almost invariably rot and die before they can be developed into plants of any size.

Division
Another easy method of increasing plants is to divide them up. This is simply done by teasing apart the mature clumps and potting them up individually in small pots filled with J.I.P.2, or a standard house plant potting compost. Although many more plants will be provided by splitting them into individual pieces, it is often better to divide the large clumps into several smaller clumps which will produce attractive plants much more rapidly. The aspidistra and cyperus are examples of plants that can be increased by division.

The parent plant should be well watered before being divided. In reasonable conditions division of plants can take place at almost any time, but it would be unwise to split up plants such as spathiphyllum while they are actually in flower.

Leaf Cuttings
For the professional, cuttings from leaves or stems of flowering and foliage plants are by far the most popular way of increasing stock. For amateur and professional the principles involved are very much the same, though the professional's approach will of necessity be on a much grander scale than the budding green-fingered amateur.

Having taken the necessary precautions to ensure that cutting material is sound, conditions are clean and temperature adequate, the next most important consideration is to ensure that the cuttings do not become dry and limp. Prospects of rooting cuttings in this condition will be very much more difficult.

The nurseryman, as mentioned earlier, has the benefit of a regular fine mist descending on his cutting beds which ensures that they remain moist without ever becoming saturated. Complete saturation of compost is undesirable, as the severed ends of cuttings are likely to begin to rot before they have had a chance to callus over and produce roots. Ideally, the propagating medium should be moistened sufficiently for one to be just able to squeeze moisture from between the fingers when a fistful of the mixture is tightly compressed.

It would be totally impractical for the average householder to rig up a mist unit indoors, unless it can be done in a spare room in a small polythened-off area with a single mist jet operating. This is quite feasible for the real enthusiast, but precautions would have to be taken to ensure that the unit is properly waterproofed. The object should be to construct

something similar to an individual shower unit, but on a smaller scale.

The point of all this is to prevent the leaves of the cutting transpiring. By keeping the area surrounding the cuttings moist, leaves will give off much less moisture and remain more turgid, giving the cutting an infinitely better chance of producing roots of its own.

By now the owner of the solitary African violet who had contemplated propagating a few leaves will have been completely discouraged by the prospect of having to go to so much bother. Take heart, there are other ways of propagating cuttings using far less sophisticated methods. The simplest method of all is to use polythene, unperforated, in which to enclose the cuttings and reduce transpiration. Half or full-sized plastic seed trays with a transparent plastic lid in which there is an adjustable ventilator are also available, and make useful propagating boxes. A further aid is the application of a small quantity of hormone rooting powder which will encourage most cuttings to root much more readily, particularly those of a hard, woody nature, such as rhoicissus and fatshedera. Severed ends of cuttings should be first dipped in water, then in the rooting powder; the powder will cling easily to the moistened cuttings.

As there are always newcomers to the pleasures of growing plants indoors it may be as well to give a run-down on the basic procedure to be followed when attempting to root cuttings. The saintpaulia is a good example of an indoor plant that can be propagated with little difficulty in the living room, or on the kitchen window-sill for that matter. All the leaves of saintpaulia will produce young plants if the cuttings and the conditions are satisfactory.

Take a clean 5-in. half pot, fill this with moist peat or J.I.P.1 compost gently pressed into position, but avoid ramming hard. Use an unperforated polythene bag about 9 to 12 in. in length into which the pot will fit comfortably; try it before preparing the cuttings just to be sure. Three canes a little shorter than the bag will also be necessary, not forgetting the rooting powder. Alternatively a plastic propagating box can be used.

From the saintpaulia select only the more mature, unblemished leaves – up to six if they can be spared, or one or two from each of several plants. These should be removed from the plant by gripping the leaf stalk firmly and bending it to one side until it breaks off at the base where it was attached to the parent plant. A knife should not be used to cut the stalk, as the piece that remains attached will in time die back and may cause the entire plant to rot and die.

So we have our six cuttings – the next move is to make six evenly spaced holes in the compost with a pencil, into which the cuttings will be placed. Avoid making the holes too deep, as it is essential that the cutting should come into contact with the compost at the bottom of the hole. Holes about 1½ in. in depth should be sufficient for the majority of cuttings.

The next step is to dip each cutting in turn in water, then in the rooting powder, before inserting them in the prepared holes. In order to keep the leaves reasonably upright the peat should be gently firmed with the fingers around each cutting in turn. The three canes are then pushed into the compost at even spacing around the edge of the pot. We are often told that the cuttings should be well watered in, but this is not really necessary if the compost is fairly moist to begin with.

Follow this by placing the plant pot in the bottom of the polythene bag and drawing the bag up over the top of the three canes. The top of the bag is then drawn together and a piece of tape used to make the bag completely airtight. The inside of the bag will quite quickly mist up as a result of condensation, but this should not cause undue concern as the cuttings will be perfectly all right inside. It will be necessary to remove, or at least to open, the bag about once each week to check that everything is in order. Any cutting that shows signs of rotting must be removed immediately and the area

Taking leaf cuttings of saintpaulias. It is important to select firm, unblemished leaves

Opposite, top: *Saxifraga sarmentosa,* known as mother-of-thousands because of the many runners it produces, is another easily propagated plant

Bottom: Pineapples can be propagated by cutting off the tufted top of the fruit and pressing it into a shallow bed of sand over a peaty compost

Peperomia caperata is another plant which can be increased from leaf cuttings in a similar way to saintpaulias

Opposite: *Ananas bracteatus striatus*, the variegated pineapple, *Hedera helix* Chicago, *Begonia rex* and, in the background, *Rhoicissus rhomboidea*

surrounding the cutting hole should be treated with an anti-fungus powder to prevent the rot spreading to other cuttings in the pot.

The potful of cuttings should be kept in a warm room, avoiding direct sunlight, and a steady temperature in the region of 18°C. (65°F.) should be maintained. Depending on conditions cuttings will have begun to root in some four to six weeks. After four weeks one should be able to leave the top of the polythene bag open, or if in a propagating box to open the ventilator, and after six weeks the bag or lid can be removed altogether.

During the six-week period the owner will have been tempted many times to dig up the cuttings to see what, if anything, is going on below soil level. This is a temptation that should be resisted, as any disturbance of developing young roots will inevitably result in a setback. However, should the temptation be too much we could perhaps permit the removal of one cutting, since the others will all be making similar progress. To remove the cutting it would be wise first to water the compost, then use a teaspoon to get the cutting out with a reasonable amount of compost attached, so causing the minimum amount of disturbance. When you are satisfied that the cutting is doing well and roots are showing through the compost, the cutting should be carefully replaced and left un-

disturbed to allow its further development.

While cuttings are developing to the stage where well-formed clusters of new leaves are evident round the stalk of the parent plant, keep the compost moist by occasionally watering with tepid water, being careful not to saturate it.

By the time the cuttings are mature enough for transferring into individual pots, the compost should be well filled with roots. Before potting up the cuttings, the compost should be watered until the water drains freely through the holes in the bottom of the pot. Then, by carefully spacing the fingers of one hand between the cuttings, the pot can be inverted and gently knocked on the edge of a table or bench, so allowing the compost and potful of cuttings to come easily away from the pot. Each leaf cutting should be gently separated in turn with as much compost attached to the roots as possible.

At this point there are two alternative courses. Each entire cluster of young plantlets and parent leaf can be potted up into $3\frac{1}{2}$-in. pots to produce plants of reasonable size in six to nine months. The alternative is to separate the clusters of young plants into individual plantlets, each with little more than two leaves – careful handling at this stage is essential. These should then be spaced out in shallow pots or trays filled with recommended saintpaulia compost, leaving about 1 in. of space between each plantlet. Indoors it will take at the very least twelve months to produce reasonably sized plants by this method, but they will be very much more attractive than those produced from potting up clumps of plants. By the latter method plants develop masses of untidy, overlapping leaves through which flowers poke their way in every direction. The slower method of producing plants ensures that the plant has a single crown and all growth radiates from the centre, and flowers when they appear stand up much more attractively from the centre of the plant well clear of the leaves.

Up until the time the young plants are ready for potting this procedure may be followed for the majority of plants to be propagated from cuttings indoors. The difference lies in the treatment of the young plants.

Other simple plants that can be propagated from leaf cuttings in a similar way to the saintpaulia are the peperomias, in particular *P. caperata* and *P. hederaefolia*. However, there is no need to divide the clumps of young plants when they have rooted and are ready for potting up. *Peperomia sandersii* is another that may be increased from leaves; the method here, however, is if anything more interesting. Instead of utilising the complete leaf, it is divided into four equal sections down and across. The

quartered pieces are then inserted upright in
the compost just far enough for them to remain
erect. Agreed, more care is required in order to
succeed, but it is fascinating when perfectly
shaped young plants appear along the edge of the
quartered cutting at the point of insertion in the
compost.

The Rex begonias are equally interesting in
this respect, and the newcomer to house plants
is often loath to believe that new plants can be
made from cutting leaves up into squares little
more than the size of a postage stamp and placing

them face upwards on moist peat. On seeing
these small leaf sections with young plants
attached for the first time the incredulous onlooker may well associate it with some form of
black magic.

Here again, like from like plays its part –
good cuttings or leaves mean good plants – and
provided you have clean accessories, an adequate
temperature of 18°C. (65°F.) and good light,
who knows, you may well succeed. It will be an
advantage if additional artificial light can be
provided for *B. rex* cuttings during the winter
months when natural daylight is inadequate for
good results.

Besides cutting leaves into sections the Rex
type of begonia can also be increased by removing complete leaves, preferably unblemished, and cutting across the large veins of
the leaves with a sharp knife or razor blade. The
leaf is then placed face uppermost on moist peat
or cutting compost in a similar fashion to the
smaller sections. A few pebbles should be placed
on top of the leaf to weigh it down, or it can be
pegged down with a hairpin to ensure that it is
in close contact with the compost. Curling up
of the leaf through drying out of the compost
will almost certainly result in failure.

A slight variation is needed when propagating
the more difficult *B. masoniana* (iron cross).
Here the leaf should be cut up into sections

some 2 in. by 1½ in. in size with a slight taper towards the leaf stalk. The slightly pointed end is then inserted in the compost. Propagating conditions are exactly the same; the iron cross begonia cuttings take a little longer to respond to care and attention.

Top or Stem Cuttings

Almost all the house plants of taller habit which produce growing stems from which branches and leaves emerge can be propagated by means of top or stem cuttings. A top cutting is the end part of the growth, and with many types of plants (the aphelandra is a good example) it provides the best cutting, while other plants produce growth at the top that is often too soft to be of any real value. Stem cuttings are prepared from single leaves with a piece of stem attached, or simply from the piece of stem as in the case of dieffenbachias. Often enough, with hederas for example, three or four leaves with a longer piece of stem will be used. In these instances it is usually advisable to remove the lower leaf or two and not to bury the remaining leaves in the compost. Plants resulting from this type of cutting are often fuller and of better quality.

In the case of cuttings with smaller leaves (hederas, tradescantias and *Ficus pumila*) it is advisable to insert as many as six cuttings in a 3½-in. pot. Plants so produced are of much better appearance than those from only one or two cuttings in each pot. Hederas, being easy to propagate, should be inserted directly into the compost in which they are expected to grow – transferring them from peat to compost is not necessary with the easier plants, and causes unnecessary disturbance of the new root system. However, when rooting cuttings of the larger leaved hederas such as *H. canariensis* they should first be encouraged to root in peat.

There are a great number of easy and difficult indoor plants that may be increased in very much the same way as the hederas, or ivies. For the more difficult plants a generally higher temperature will be required to encourage root development.

Crotons, for example, because of their highly coloured foliage and tropical origin, are difficult plants to manage indoors if they do not have adequate temperature and a very light position in which to grow. Yet, when propagated from top cuttings 4 to 6 in. in length, they root quite readily in ideal conditions. If need be cuttings of croton can be very much longer and still root with reasonable ease. It may be helpful to know this, so that one can establish new plants of reasonably good quality from apparently poor parent plants.

Crotons are notorious for shedding their lower leaves and growing tufts of foliage on otherwise bare stems. To produce acceptable plants from such a parent the cutting should be removed with about 5 in. of bare stem attached. With a sharp knife make notches along the stem in five or six places that will be below soil level when the cutting is inserted, and treat the notches and severed end of the stem with a rooting powder. Prepare a potful of J.I.P.2 compost pressed down fairly firmly and make a reasonably large hole with a dibber into which moist sphagnum peat should be gently pressed in with the dibber. The cutting is then inserted in the peat far enough for the leaves to come into contact with the surface of the compost. Cover the pot with a polythene bag as recommended earlier. You may be quite surprised at the good results and the amount of root that develops, not only from the severed end, but all the way along the section of stem that is below soil level at the points where notches were made.

This is not the sort of propagating method that appeals to the professional, but it does have many advantages for the amateur. A final point: when cutting the stems of crotons care should be taken to ensure that the sap does not get onto one's clothing – from personal experience I have regrettably learned that the stain is impossible to remove.

The rubber plant, *Ficus elastica robusta*, may be propagated in a number of ways, leaf and top cuttings being the most practical. Cuttings are best taken while plants are dormant, usually between the months of November and March. The propagating bed temperature requires to be rather high, something in excess of 21°C. (70°F.) for best results. Very soft cuttings with large leaves rarely do well; firm cuttings with some three or four leaves attached do very much better. (With any form of top cutting it is important to ensure that there are at least two firm leaves on the stem, otherwise it will all be a waste of time). Stem cuttings of rubber plants are prepared by cutting the stem of the plant up into sections of 1½ to 2 in. in length with a leaf stalk in the centre of each piece of stem. The parent leaf should be left attached to the stem section until such time as the plant is ready for potting into its final container for that year. The leaf is carefully cut away below soil level with a sharp knife – no harm is suffered by the cutting which by then is well established on its own root system, deriving little or no benefit from the parent leaf which played such an important part when young roots were in the process of development. Other ways of propagating rubber plants are described in the A to Z chapter, and on page 64.

Stem cuttings of hederas, which root easily, can be inserted directly into the compost in which they will grow

Opposite:
Fuchsia, *Tradescantia purpurea* (centre), *Philodendron melanochrysum* and, in the foreground, *Stromanthe amabilis* and *Ficus radicans variegata*, the variegated trailing fig

A stem cutting of *Ficus elastica* with its leaf attached. It can be seen that it has rooted well into the compost and produced a new shoot

Stem cuttings prepared without the usual leaves can also provide a source of interest and wonderment to the casual observer. Dieffenbachias, those attractive members of the aroid family, can, as mentioned earlier, be propagated in this way, some of them from quite large trunks. These are generally slower to root; the wonder is that they root at all. A word of warning though; croton sap will stain one's clothing, but the sap of the dumb cane has a very different effect. The common name of 'dumb cane' may give a clue; should the sap of this plant get onto one's tongue it will cause unpleasant swelling that will make speech difficult for several days. The sap also smells very unpleasantly which is enough to deter anyone from putting it near, far less into, the mouth.

On most varieties stems will, quite naturally, become leafless and woody in time. When this happens and the plant is no longer attractive the stems should be cut to within a few inches from their base. Keep the potful of stumps as they usually grow again from the base. The stems can then be cut up into sections some 2 to 3 in. in length. After dusting the ends with rooting powder the cuttings should be pressed horizontally into a seed box filled with moist peat until the pieces of stem are almost covered. Any growth buds (small swellings on the stem) that can be seen should be uppermost. As soon as the first two leaves have opened, pot into $3\frac{1}{2}$-in. size pots. Many dracaenas (*D*. Rededge in particular), and philodendrons with larger leaves can also be propagated in exactly the same way.

Dracaena massangeana is one of the more impressive foliage plants though space demanding, but good value if the room can be afforded. When freely planted in beds of compost or when growing in their natural habitat they become quite substantial plants. Any house plant grower who can acquire an old stem of one of these more mature plants can intrigue his friends by propagating stout stems several inches in diameter on the window-sill with few problems. The cutting (if you can call a small tree trunk a cutting) is placed the correct way up (preferably) in a saucer of water. Roots develop in the water, leaves appear on the stem and you have a plant that will go on for quite a time with virtually no attention other than replenishment of the water. It will, of course, in time have to be potted up into a proper growing medium.

Root Cuttings
Dracaenas also produce thumb-thick root growths that can be removed by taking the plant out of its pot and cutting them away with a sharp knife. Cut into inch-long sections, these pieces root with little bother if buried in pots or boxes

of moist peat – no elaborate propagating paraphernalia is required. Cuttings should be potted up into J.I.P.2 about two weeks after new growth has pushed up through the soil.

Air-layering

A number of indoor plants may be propagated by this method, and it is also an excellent way of reducing the height of rubber plants which are getting out of hand.

Plants are air-layered simply by removing a section of the outer bark and wrapping a handful of wet sphagnum moss around the exposed area, or by making an upward cut through the main stem and wrapping wet sphagnum moss round the incision.

First remove a leaf at about the height you wish the new plant to be; the section of stem above this point should have at least three or four mature leaves. Make a cut halfway through the main stem about 1 in. below the joint of the leaf you have removed, bringing the cut up vertically through the actual node. A piece of matchstick inserted in the opening will hold it open and, after dusting it with hormone rooting powder, wrap the incision in a handful of wet sphagnum moss. This in turn should be wrapped in polythene which is tied firmly in position above and below the moss, the object being to exclude the air and prevent it drying out.

Plants will vary in the time they take to produce new roots into the moss, but when a good supply of healthy white roots can be seen through the polythene the stem can be cleanly severed a little below the moss ball. Let the cut end dry, remove the polythene and, leaving the moss ball intact, pot the new plant into a pot of its own, using a peaty compost. Water in, then keep on the dry side during the first few weeks to encourage root development.

In time the lower part of the old plant will develop new growth at several points near the top of the stem.

Finally, it is again emphasised that to be successful in producing new plants from old, good plant material, adequate temperature and lightly shaded, hygienic conditions are the most important requirements.

Air-layering a ficus. The incision is bound with moist moss covered with clear polythene and tied firmly top and bottom to prevent it drying out

The few plant troubles

The first lesson to be learned here is that in order to control or eliminate pests on house plants some form of insecticide is usually necessary, and the lesson is that care must be exercised when handling and storing any form of insecticide. Keeping them in a safe place away from children, and very often adults too, is of prime importance. For the majority such advice may seem unnecessary, but it is worth recalling that an ever-increasing number of people inadvertently drink weedkiller or other poison annually with fatal results.

Fortunately, the majority of really poisonous insecticides are not available to the general public, but even those that are considered safe should be handled carefully. Certainly, when handling insecticides rubber gloves should be worn as general practice, and any plants that need treatment, particularly with a liquid solution that is sprayed on, should be treated out of doors. Although many of these sprays are harmless they do have an unpleasant odour, which is ample reason in itself for treating plants in the open air, and they may well be fatal to a cage bird or small animal if used in the confined space of a room.

In the garden it is better to choose a shaded spot for dealing with pot plants, and a still, warm day is preferable. When applying an insecticide as a spray it is of prime importance to ensure that all the foliage of the plant is saturated, particularly the undersides of leaves where the majority of pests such as red spider and scale insects are to be found.

A further precaution is to ensure that the insecticide manufacturer's instructions for preparation and use of his product are followed to the letter. Often enough only a small amount of the solution is required, but it is better to mix the minimum amount stipulated by the manufacturer and dispose of any surplus rather than experiment with hit-and-miss smaller quantities in the belief that one is being economical. In almost every aspect of plant growing excess can be dangerous, and this is never more so than in the use of pest controls. Mixing insecticides to excessive strength may indeed put paid to the pest, but there is no benefit if the plant should succumb in the process.

In common with earlier suggestions for applying a new leaf cleaning product to only one leaf in order to test reaction, the same should apply with insecticides. Test them on a section of the plant if there is any doubt and allow a week or ten days for any reaction before treating the entire plant. Better to be safe than sorry.

This may seem a rather doleful manner in which to start a new chapter and, possibly, enough to put some readers off growing indoor plants for all time. Relax; it is not nearly so dreadful as the foregoing may suggest. In actual fact the house plant grower is not too much troubled by pests, and if you follow my earlier suggestion about purchasing plants from a reliable source then the chance of introducing pests to your collection of plants is further reduced. The majority of nurserymen exercise a rigid programme of pest control so that their plants may be offered to the customer in a clean, healthy condition. Even so, it is inevitable that some pests will escape the net, hence the need for care when choosing your plants.

When purchasing, a brief inspection of the plant is advisable. The majority of pests are easily discernible with the naked eye, and a glance at the undersides of leaves may well change your mind about a proposed purchase. Inspection of the growing tips of hederas, for example, will often show colonies of greenfly feasting there. Greenfly should be looked for on buds and flowers of flowering plants – the hibiscus is a good example of a flowering plant which is vulnerable to greenfly attack. They may also be found under the leaves as well as on new growth, where they are very easily detected.

Another seasonal pest is whitefly which can be easily seen on the undersides of leaves if the plant is turned upside down for inspection, or they will be seen dancing away if the plant is gently shaken. Badly affected plants should be avoided, but the odd few whitefly are not particularly harmful, though one would not wish to introduce them to a situation where other plants would become hosts to the unwanted beasties.

Scale insects are small, limpet-like insects that cling to plant stems, underneath leaves, and in particularly bad attacks may also be found on leaf surfaces. The adults of these are dark brown in colour while the young ones are flesh coloured. A mild attack of scale is not too damaging, but if left unchecked they multiply quite rapidly and will completely cripple the plant in time. They also leave a sticky deposit on leaves and stems which does nothing to improve their appearance.

Mealy bug is another pest that may be encountered. Not very particular about which part of the plant he inhabits, he does have a penchant for finding his way between twisting stems and overlapping leaves where he can be particularly inaccessible to any pest control that may be used. One consolation is that mealy

Though the flowers of *Hibiscus rosa-sinensis* are superb, like many flowering plants the hibiscus is vulnerable to greenfly attack

bugs are not difficult to see, as they wrap their young in a cotton wool-like substance. Adult bugs are very similar to small wood lice and powdery white in colour.

Another pest that is, fortunately, not so prevalent today is tarsonemid mite. Very minute, invisible to the naked eye, they concentrate their activities mainly on new young growth, ivies being one of their favourite hosts. Distorted and leafless young growth is an indication of their presence. Unfortunately, there is little one can do to eradicate, or even control these pests, as the one effective chemical is highly poisonous and not available to the general public. Drastic though it may appear, the only sensible course when mite presence has been confirmed is to dispose of the plant, so reducing the chance of the trouble spreading and other plants in the vicinity becoming affected.

Possibly one of the most destructive of all the pests is the minute red spider mite which, on account of its size, is one of the most difficult pests for the untrained eye to detect. Not very particular about which plants should receive their attentions, red spider can be found on garden plants and trees as well as many of the plants used for indoor decoration. Alas, they frequently go undiscovered until they have taken a strong hold and considerably weakened the plant, so making the task of control all the more difficult.

They can be seen with a small magnifying glass mostly on the undersides of leaves, and pin-prick holes in the leaf are an indication that red spider mites are present. Red spider seem particularly partial to some plants, of which *Hedera canariensis* is one. When spider is well established small criss-crossing webs can be seen on the undersides of leaves, and as they drain the sap from the plant the leaves become light brown at the edges and the plant takes on a generally dry and hard appearance. Where the growing conditions are very hot and dry the risk of red spider becoming a nuisance is very much increased.

Finally, a pest that attacks the roots of plants is root mealy bug. It is not often encountered but is sometimes seen on plants which remain in the same pots for long periods, bromeliads being good examples. *Aralia elegantissima* is another.

The mood of despondency in the house plant grower must by now be almost complete at the prospect of having so many wee beasties crawling

Hedera canariensis, shown here, is prone to attack by red spider mites, especially in very hot, dry conditions

about the house. Let me again assert that it would be most unusual and something of a disaster for all these to be present, and the chances are that one is likely to come across nothing more than the occasional attack of greenfly. The foregoing information on pests is intended to make their detection easier and the ensuing advice, it is hoped, will help to keep them under control.

Greenfly (Aphids)

These are comparatively easy to eradicate, there being many brands of insecticide on the market that will quickly eliminate them. Larger plants can only be treated by thoroughly spraying the entire plant and repeating the process as necessary. Smaller plants, on the other hand, can be dealt with equally effectively by plunging the plant in a bucketful of prepared insecticide. Do this by wrapping a piece of polythene around the pot so that the soil cannot spill out, then dip the plant in the insecticide and swish it around to ensure that all leaves and stems have been well saturated, not forgetting first to don rubber gloves. Keep the plant out of the sun and allow the foliage to dry naturally before replacing in position.

Whitefly

A very different kettle of fish and one of the most difficult pests to clear up completely once they have got a hold. There are all sorts of insecticides available but not all of them, by any means, are effective. The owner of smaller plants affected by whitefly may well benefit from the advice I was given by an old nurseryhand who has lived with the business all his life. His way of clearing up whitefly is simple, inexpensive and very effective. He merely seals the entire plant in a polythene bag in a similar way to home-grown cuttings for twenty four hours. The result is a clean plant and some very dead whitefly. Try it; you will be surprised at the effectiveness of this method. I certainly was.

Scale

These are rather messy pests, when they have got a firm hold on a plant, but not particularly difficult to eradicate. They can be thoroughly sprayed or submerged, in just the same way as suggested for greenfly control, in a solution of malathion insecticide. Treatment would have to be repeated at intervals of about ten days to ensure that young and adult mites are eliminated. Possibly a more effective treatment that need only be done once if done thoroughly is to soak a sponge in malathion solution and to wipe off the scale. A gentle dab with the sponge will be of no use; they attach themselves quite firmly,

so a little pressure is required to wipe them off.

A few of the plants that scale insects seem particularly partial to are aphelandra, *Aralia elegantissima*, *Asplenium nidus* and *Citrus mitis*.

Mealy Bug

Another pest that ruins the appearance of affected plants. Easy to detect but, as mentioned earlier, very difficult to kill off completely once they have made a home in the tangled branches of such climbing plants as stephanotis and hoya.

One is often invited to visit the greenhouse of an enthusiastic amateur and see the wonderful range of plants being cultivated under one roof. Many of these plant collections are managed extremely well but often enough an incredible infestation of mealy bug will be shrugged off with the comment, 'Of course, there is a bit of bug about.' The sad part of it all is that a thorough drenching spray regularly repeated would lead to considerable improvement.

There are many insecticides available for the control of mealy bug – some better than others. The most important requirement when treating plants against this pest is to ensure contact, so a very thorough, drenching spray is essential. Otherwise it is a complete waste of effort.

For the odd smaller patch of bug the time-honoured treatment of dabbing them with a small brush, or piece of cotton wool, soaked in methylated spirit is quite effective.

The important thing with these pests, as with all others, is to keep on top of them, as they are much more of a problem once they have become established. The good grower practises a policy of prevention rather than cure – possibly a simpler task on the nursery than in the living room or kitchen. But it does, nevertheless, pay to keep a watchful eye for unwanted visitors on one's plants.

Red Spider Mite

A fortune must be spent annually by growers of all sorts of plants in their efforts to keep this wee mite under control, so there is no lack of material when choosing an insecticide with which to treat them. It would be foolish to list the insecticides that are available as they are changing and, we are told, being improved upon all the time. The helpful plant retailer will be the best person to consult in order to obtain advice on the current popular product. Thereafter, follow the manufacturer's directions, and be sure to thoroughly saturate the undersides of plant leaves. In order to discourage attack from red spider a moist environment should be maintained around the plants and dry atmosphere and arid conditions should be avoided.

Some common mistakes

Questions following talks on indoor plants, countless letters seeking advice and ailing plants brought in for inspection have provided ample material for this chapter. Much of it has already been dealt with, however, in other parts of the book so I will just highlight some of the most common causes of failure in the raising of indoor plants.

Growing plants in difficult, dark locations account for many failures. The symptoms are discolouration and eventual loss of leaves, and production of small leaves on woody, thin stems. In very dark situations new leaves would be something of a luxury.

Excessive heat should be guarded against as this will also frequently result in poor, weedy growth – rubber plant leaves droop miserably in very hot conditions. Keep plants away from radiators and out of the stream of hot air rising from them. If plants must be placed on heating appliances the shelf width should be increased to ensure that rising hot air is deflected away from plants and not through their leaves.

When using aerosol sprays of any description (other than those for pest control and cleaning) plants should be carefully avoided; better still to remove them from the room altogether.

For plants other than those one is advised to keep permanently wet, complete saturation of the compost for long periods will prove harmful. Plants should dry out a little between each watering, but excessive drying out of the compost should also be guarded against as this condition can be equally damaging.

The majority of plants will do better if watered with rain water, which for preference should be applied at room temperature. Very cold water can prove fatal to such plants as saintpaulia.

When experimenting with new products they should be tried on one plant, or part of a plant, in order to test the reaction. It is much better to be safe than sorry.

The majority of plants will do perfectly well (in spite of views to the contrary) in rooms heated by gas appliances provided the atmosphere does not become stuffy; this means that the rooms should be ventilated daily. Draughts can be harmful to many plants, but fresh air on a warm day can do a power of good.

Plants need to be fed when established in their pots, but one should resist the temptation to overdo it as excessive feeding can often be more harmful than no feeding at all. Abide by the fertiliser manufacturer's instructions and better results will be obtained.

Pot plants on when needed but avoid the tendency to put plants into pots that are much too large in relation to their size. Use pots only a little larger, and procure a properly balanced potting compost. It is seldom, if ever, that one sees good-quality plants growing in what is often referred to as garden dirt. Composts should contain peat, sand, fertiliser and all sorts of other ingredients if potted plants are to do well.

When introducing new plants to a collection, whether they be gifts or purchased, a brief inspection should be made for the presence of pests, as these are very much easier to avoid than to eradicate.

Like fertilisers, all insecticides should be used as instructed, as that seemingly harmless little extra may well cause leaf scorch and other damage. Pests should be treated as soon as they are seen, as any delay will make their control just that much more difficult.

Calathea zebrina
requires warm, shady
conditions – not a
plant to choose for a
sunny but unheated
room

71

A to Z
list of
house
plants

ABUTILON

**South America. 10 to 13°C. (50 to 55°F.).
Year round. Easy.**

These shrubby plants are best suited to the cool, lightly shaded garden room, rather than indoor conditions. Keep well watered during the active growing period in spring and summer, and on the dry side at other times. It is mostly hybrid forms which are offered for sale. Producing maple-like leaves and pendulous bell-shaped flowers, abutilons may be used as centre pieces in outdoor bedding schemes during the summer months. If pruned in September–October they will require less winter storage space. Stems can be shortened by half their length to keep plants in shape.

Propagate from seed sown early in the year, or from easily rooted cuttings taken at the same time. As plants become established, pinch out the leading growth to encourage a more compact appearance.

ACALYPHA HISPIDA (Red-hot Cat's Tails or Chenille Plant)

**New Guinea. 16 to 21°C. (60 to 70°F.).
Difficult.**

Not easy to care for indoors, *Acalypha hispida* requires a constant temperature and humid conditions to succeed. It is perfectly suited to the area surrounding a water feature in the spacious greenhouse or garden room; the long beetroot-red 'cats' tails' hanging over the water will be reflected and set off to very good effect. In ideal conditions the plant will attain a height of some 8 to 10 ft. but can be kept in check by pruning at almost any time, so there is no need to fear an invasion.

There are a number of other acalyphas, but the *hispida* kind is the most spectacular. All are susceptible to attack by red spider mite, so a careful watch must be kept for this troublesome pest. Propagation is best effected by means of cuttings taken in the early spring.

Abutilon Fireball

ACHIMENES (Hot-water Plant)

Mexico, Brazil. 10 to 18°C. (50 to 65°F.). Easy.

Compact flowering plants which do well in a light window. The amusing common name is derived from the fact that growth from scaly rhizomes can be induced to break more freely if the pot is plunged into hot water during February, following the dormant winter period. Water sparingly while growth is developing, more freely when the plant is in full leaf. When plants die back naturally in the autumn water should be gradually withheld. Keep warm and dry throughout the winter.

Increase by seed sown in February–March, from which a wide assortment of flower colours should result. Cuttings of both leaf and stem can be rooted in April, or the scaly rhizomes can be gently teased apart and planted up individually in February. With so many alternative methods of propagation there should be little

Left: Achimenes

Bottom: *Acalypha hispida*

Opposite: *Scindapsus
aureus* Marble Queen
(left foreground),
*Dracaena deremensis
rhoersii, Caladium* Red
Flare, *Caladium
candidum* and, in the
centre, the creeping
fig, *Ficus pumila*

excuse for failure. If larger plants are required, young plants can be potted on into larger containers as soon as they have become established in smaller pots.

ACORUS GRAMINEUS

Japan. Hardy. Easy.

A grass-like plant with congested cream and green leaves, which enjoys very moist conditions. Beside the indoor pool is the best location or, if an indoor pool is out of the question, the plants can be grown equally well if the growing pot is placed in a 3-in. deep pot saucer kept filled with water.

The acorus is frequently used by florists and nurserymen when planting bowls or dish gardens, as the stiff, grassy foliage blends well with most planting schemes. However, on buying such gardens the purchaser should ensure that the other plants in the arrangement also prefer moist conditions. Acorus are hardy out of doors, but plants bought from a house-plant supplier would require to be well hardened off before planting in the open, and the best time to plant out would be in mid-summer. Plants are easily increased by division of the roots at almost any time. Start the divided pieces in peat, then transfer to J.I.P.2 compost, or similar.

ADIANTUM (Maidenhair Fern)

South America, Australia and New Zealand. 10 to 18°C. (50 to 65°F.). Moderately easy.

There are many varieties of adiantum to choose from, all of them delicately beautiful, reasonably easy to care for and supremely adaptable. Plant them in dish or bowl gardens, as individuals to stand on top of a pedestal, or in hanging baskets. To see them at their best the latter method cannot be bettered.

When creating a display, be it in the fireplace or at the flower club, there can be few plants that blend in so readily with almost any chosen colour scheme. And one cannot imagine any major function at which flowers play an important part where cut maidenhair fern would not be used in quantity. To supply adiantum for this purpose the nurseryman forsakes pot culture and plants his stock into specially prepared beds in the ground in his greenhouses, which gives a greatly increased yield. The owner of the garden room may well benefit from the nurseryman's example by planting adiantum at the front of prepared beds containing an assortment of house plants.

A shaded position is preferred. Water freely other than during the winter months when permanently wet compost can be harmful. Propagate by division. A sharp knife will be required to cut through the matted roots of older clumps. When split, the smaller clumps should be potted up individually and watered in. Less congested clumps can be teased apart into smaller, or even individual, pieces if a large number of new plants are required.

The more ambitious house plant grower can often proudly claim to being green fingered by propagating new adiantums from spores. There always seems to be an aura of mystique about this means of increasing plants, yet it is not so difficult provided a warm, shaded propagator and moist conditions can be provided. Spores develop on the undersides of fronds and should be allowed to remain on the plant until they become dusty and fall from the leaf when tapped. At this stage the leaf should be cut away from the plant and placed in a paper bag, which in turn is placed on top of a warm radiator. Some 24 hours later the majority of spores will have dislodged themselves quite naturally and can be lightly sown on the surface of fine, moist peat, with a little sand added. In good conditions, with the essential bit of luck required, a soft green carpet of minute maidenhair ferns should be produced. When large enough to handle they can be potted into small pots of peaty compost, several pieces to each pot. Transfer into larger containers as necessary.

There are also hardy and more tender species available, but those offered for home decoration are, generally speaking, a middle-of-the-road selection which will do better indoors.

AECHMEA (Urn Plant)

Brazil. 16 to 18°C. (60 to 65°F.). Year round. Easy.

Only two aechmeas are generally available and one of those, *Aechmea fulgens*, only infrequently as supplies are very limited. *A. rhodocyanea* (previously *A. fasciata*) is the more attractive and has, in recent years, become an important house plant, particularly in the higher price range. *A. fulgens* is much the smaller of the two, and has burgundy-coloured foliage. The dark blue flowers are short lived, but the bract that emerges from the centre of the rosette will remain colourful for two months or more.

A. rhodocyanea is one of the most exotic and unusual of all potted plants. Large, strap-like overlapping leaves form a perfectly watertight urn (hence the common name). When purchasing, look for plants with lighter grey colouring as the darker ones are less attractive.

To prevent damage to the natural grey bloom on the leaves it is important to ensure that they are not cleaned or rubbed in any way.

When buying plants in flower it is best to select those that are more backward in order to get the longest life possible from them. The ideal stage is when the pink bract is a little above the water level in the urn. Plants that have developed to the stage where the blue flowers in the otherwise pink bract are fully open should be avoided. Though expensive, if purchased at the proper stage of development, *A. rhodocyanea* will give anything from eight to ten months of pleasure before the bract eventually deteriorates. The high cost merely reflects the time taken by the nurseryman to bring the plant to maturity, at least five years from seed under normal conditions. The time can be reduced by adding carefully controlled amounts of chemical to the water in the reservoir, but it is not the sort of treatment that can be recommended to the householder owning just one or two plants.

Aechmeas belong to the bromeliad family, and an essential part of their culture is to ensure that the water reservoir formed by the leaves is kept permanently topped up with water. This may take on an unpleasant odour in time, and it is therefore advisable to change the water completely every six weeks or so. Only a little water requires to be given to the actual compost, so that it is just moist and never saturated.

The compost used when potting must be of an open, fibrous nature incorporating a good amount of leafmould and peat. Aechmeas, if well grown, become large and top heavy, and must be potted into clay pots in order to prevent them overbalancing. When using clay pots for any plants it is important to ensure that a good layer of crocks is placed in the bottom of the pot to assist drainage and prevent waterlogging.

The least rewarding aspect of bromeliad cultivation is the fact that each rosette produces a colourful bract only once and then dies. We get many questions on this subject, but nothing whatever can be done to prevent what is, after all, a completely natural part of the plant's life cycle. Therefore a little advice is necessary on the best procedure to adopt when the bract and the rosette is no longer attractive.

Firstly, the stem of the flower should be cut through at about water level with a sharp knife. If the bract shows signs of disintegrating it will be found that the entire flower stalk can be removed if it is pulled gently while the rosette is held in position. Frequently the main rosette will remain attractive for a few weeks longer, by which time a cluster of new young plantlets (or just one if you are unlucky) will have begun to form at the base of the parent rosette. Again,

a sharp knife should be used to remove the old plant when it has lost its appearance, the cut being made just above the small plants to avoid damaging them.

A choice is then open: the young plants can be removed when large enough (when they have at least five leaves) and potted individually, or they can be left attached to grow as a cluster on the parent root stump. When adopting the latter method new bracts will develop in much less time than when plants are treated individually. If plantlets are to be potted up singly the plant must be removed from its pot so that they can be separated together with any roots that have formed.

If fresh seed is available it will be found that bromeliads are not difficult to raise in this way.

AESCHYNANTHUS

South East Asia. Minimum 16°C. (60°F.). Difficult.

Indoors it would be difficult to create the dank, humid conditions that these exotic relations of the columnea require. However, for the fortunate few who can provide the minimum temperature suggested and the humidity created by frequent damping of the area surrounding the plant, it can be most rewarding. The maximum temperature is not important provided conditions are shaded and moist.

Propagate by cuttings about 5 in. in length, preferably in spring, but non-flowering top cuttings should present little difficulty at any time provided there is a warm, close atmosphere in which to house them.

When cuttings have become established, pot them up in $3\frac{1}{2}$-in. pots using a mixture of equal parts J.I.P.2 compost and coarse peat. Following this the cuttings may be treated in various ways, but one has only to see them form a well-filled hanging basket to realise that this is by far the best effect likely to be achieved. After a few weeks in the $3\frac{1}{2}$-in. pots they can be transferred to the baskets, but don't skimp the job – put at least five potfuls in the basket. This will ensure a full and colourful display in the minimum length of time. With only a single plant in the basket there is an interminable wait for results; you may even miss the season altogether!

There are a number of different varieties available in glowing colours of scarlet and orange. Many of the flowers produce the purest nectar, which always interest visitors who are invited to taste it when it is shaken from a flower into their upturned palm. Compost must be kept moist at all times during the spring and summer months, and just a little dryer in

79

winter. Weak liquid fertiliser should be given frequently to established plants. When baskets of plants become hard and unattractive they should be disposed of and a fresh basket planted up, after first ensuring that there is a supply of new young plants growing on for this purpose.

AGLAONEMA

South East Asia. 16 to 21°C. (60 to 70°F.). Difficult.

Temperatures of less than 16°C. (60°F.) are often advised; for a short period this may do little harm, but it is essential to provide adequate warmth if these plants are to do well. Aglaonemas are mostly of compact habit and deserve to be more popular than they are at present. Specialist nurseries list several varieties, but on the whole they tend to be neglected. A few, such as the species *Aglaonema commutatum*, have rather dull foliage, so the lack of interest may be quite understandable.

However, there are other sorts available, *A. pseudo-bracteatum* for example, that will brighten any collection of plants. Spear-shaped leaves of *A. pseudo-bracteatum* are cream and green in colour and will attain a length of some 18 to 24 in. which is inclined to make this plant somewhat less compact than the majority of aglaonemas.

A. robelinii was for many years one of the reasonably popular plants which could be purchased without too much difficulty, but this has now been superseded by *A.* Silver Queen, which, as the name suggests, has silver-grey foliage that is also compact and neat in appearance. Planted out in a bed of peaty compost in a well-heated greenhouse this plant is quite capable of developing into a fine specimen which may measure some 4 ft. across.

In pot or border the treatment for all aglaonemas is very similar: warmth, moisture and regular feeding once established. One precaution: like the aspidistra they are very susceptible to damage if leaves are cleaned with oil or other chemical concoctions, so it is wise to experiment with one or two leaves before treating the entire plant with such products in order to be on the safe side.

Spring is said to be the best time to increase plants by division of root clumps, but this can be effected at almost any time if a warm propagating case can be provided to start the divided pieces into growth as individuals. New plants may also be raised from cuttings, but the division method is much simpler if propagating facilities are limited. Shaded conditions are preferred at all times.

AMARYLLIS (Hippeastrum)

Brazil. 10 to 16°C. (50 to 60°F.). Easy.

Mother bulbs are expensive to purchase, but ease of culture and spectacular flowers make them worthwhile acquisitions. Using pots only slightly larger than the diameter of the bulb, potting up should be undertaken in the autumn, J.I.P.3 being a suitable compost. Whatever compost is used it is essential that it should be rich, and not too thin and light. Bulbs should be potted to about half their depth and, once potted, the compost must be watered sparingly until growth develops, when the amount can be increased. A light position in a cool room is ideal.

In order to obtain satisfactory results the following year it is important to continue watering and feeding the plant after the flower has died off so that the bulb may build up a food reserve. When the foliage begins to die down naturally water should be gradually withheld until the compost is quite dry. There are many schools of thought and we are often advised to keep the plant in leaf throughout the year by keeping the compost moist, but it seems that the best flowering results are obtained by allowing the plant to rest. Plants need about two months' rest from the end of August, and it is particularly important to encourage them gently into new growth, as too much water will often result in the production of early leaves at the expense of flowers.

New plants may be raised from seed, but it is a slow business, taking at least three years before flowers can be expected. New plants may also be raised vegetatively by teasing apart the scales of mature bulbs, ensuring that part of the tough section at the base of the bulb is attached, and planting them in peaty compost. A temperature in the region of 21°C. (70°F.) should be maintained. When starting mature bulbs into growth a similar high temperature is recommended.

ANANAS (Pineapple)

Tropical America. 13 to 21°C. (55 to 70°F.). Easy.

Ananas comosus is another member of the bromeliad family and is interesting as a pot plant mainly because it is sold while bearing fruit. The plant itself is not particularly attractive and is possibly one of the least beautiful of all the fascinating bromeliads. The fruit, however, is a very strong selling point as far as the nurseryman is concerned, so they are produced in reasonably large quantities annually. Treat-

Aglaonema
Silver Queen

fruit of the green ananas; instead we have a glowing pink fruit that will in time form small flowers of the most intense shade of blue at intervals from the base to the top of the fruit. In this condition, which remains for many months, it must surely rate as one of the most exciting plants in cultivation today. Alas, the fruit is rather woody and unappetising, but you cannot have everything. As the fruit loses its colour and becomes less attractive, so the parent rosette from which it emerged also deteriorates.

An open leafmould and peat mixture is usually recommended for bromeliads, but something a little heavier is wanted for ananas when potting them on into larger pots, as the plants become top heavy in light mixtures.

Propagation is effected in a slightly different way to that described for the aechmea – in fact, there are a number of methods, although not all are satisfactory. As the fruit matures (a stout cane will be needed to hold it in position) a number of young plantlets will be produced around the top of the actual fruit. Allow these to attain reasonable size before removing and placing them in a warm propagating bed of peat and sand. However, do not expect too much from this method as these young plants frequently lose all their chlorophyll and eventually rot and die.

Besides producing new shoots in this way the variegated pineapple will also develop one or more strong growths from among the leaves of the parent rosette. These make by far the best plants in the end, and should be left to make at least six strong leaves before being removed with a sharp knife, cutting close to the parent plant. A spacious propagating case will then be required to house these large and somewhat spiteful cuttings – all the ananas have vicious spines along the edges of their leaves and need careful handling.

Another propagating method is to cut away the top of the mature fruit with the tufted rosette and allow to dry before placing it firmly on top of a propagating bed, or potful of suitable propagating mixture. It will reduce the chances of rotting if the mixture is covered with a fine layer of sand on which the fruit may rest.

The sharp-edged leaves of the pineapple can be a problem when plants have to be transported to a show ground. Our way of overcoming this is to cut the bottom out of a plastic sack and draw it up around the plant from the bottom. This is also an effective method of protecting face and hands when plants are being transferred to larger containers.

For the enthusiast with a little patience this really is a plant well worth the bother of acquiring

ment and conditions are similar to those recommended for the aechmea, but the compost will require to be kept a little moister. Foliage is a dull battleship grey in colour and the fruit when produced is interesting, but not particularly appetising.

The variegated ananas is a much more exciting plant in almost every respect. The newer form, *A. bracteatus striatus*, is much more compact and colourful, consequently easier to manage indoors than the *sativus* form. In order to retain their rich colouring, which is almost entirely cream with touches of pale green, it is essential that plants should enjoy the lightest possible position. On account of the light factor plants grown entirely indoors are rarely as good as those given greenhouse or garden-room conditions. Sun protection is only necessary on the very hottest days. In good light more mature plants of three to four years of age will take on the most exciting pinkish-red colouring in the centre of the bract. With the variegated pineapples the great moment comes when, after some three or four years, a pineapple develops and begins to emerge from the centre of the rosette. The variegated form does not have the dull

and growing on to maturity. If he can get it to fruit successfully the proud owner is truly the envy of every plantsman in the neighbourhood.

ANTHURIUM

South America. Minimum 16°C. (60°F.). Moderately easy and difficult.

The house plant grower is only likely to come into contact with the anthuriums listed below and, of these, only the last mentioned is suitable for indoor cultivation. For preference they all require very hot, humid conditions, which will mean a temperature consistently higher than that stated above. In fact, the hotter the conditions the better, provided a moist atmosphere can be maintained by regular damping of the greenhouse or garden room. The plant grower who can spare the greenhouse only a few minutes' attention before departing for work in the morning should not expect the sort of results that can be achieved by the man who can devote his time to their care. Nevertheless, much can be done with the enlistment of a willing wife who is at home all day and can be entrusted with the task of providing the essential humidity by damping around heating pipes, paths and such like.

Anthurium crystallinum is grown purely for its truly superb leaves. This is a plant which the beginner would do well to ignore until he has acquired some degree of skill with simpler subjects. In the greenhouse collections of many enthusiasts some surprisingly fine plants are grown, but it is seldom, if ever, that reasonable specimens of *A. crystallinum* are seen. Frequently the reason for this is that the grower tends to care for these plants by potting them very conventionally in standard pots, when it is infinitely better to grow them on a moss-covered raft. This is simply made from a slatted wood base, covered with a layer of good sphagnum moss; the plant is then placed in the centre of the moss and more moss is built up around the roots to the neck of the plant. Stiff wire bent in the fashion of hairpins will hold the moss in position. As roots appear through the moss the procedure is to add fresh moss as required, so there is no need for conventional potting. It will help if the moss is soaked in fertiliser solution overnight before using. As the plant outgrows the

83

raft it is a simple business to construct a larger base on to which the existing raft is placed with a layer of moss in between the two. Grown in this way in a humid greenhouse you'll have your friends believing that you have acquired some super new variety.

Again, *A. andreanum* is not a plant for the beginner, though it is seen much more often than the previous one. And if the actual plant is not familiar there is ample opportunity for seeing the flowers, which are stocked by most better class florists. The flowers have a prominent spadix with spathes that vary in colour from white to deepest red with almost every shade of exotic pink in between.

Surprisingly enough anthuriums are, on the whole, not too difficult to raise from seed provided it is fresh and sown in a temperature approaching 27°C. (80°F.). When large enough to handle the seedlings should be potted not into soil, but into a mixture of coarse peat and rough sphagnum moss; to help things along try soaking the moss in liquid fertiliser at standard strength for 24 hours before using. It is also helpful if plant pots are plunged to their rims in peat or moss beds, below which there should be permanently warm pipes, or soil-warming cables can be run through the bed. In common with most members of the aroid family this anthurium will develop aerial roots on the main stem as it extends in length. If these are left unattended to dry out in the atmosphere then the plant will suffer. To encourage these roots to provide nourishment wrap a good thick layer of fertiliser-soaked moss around the stem. Into this the roots will penetrate and improve the plant considerably. At most only three or four flowers are produced each year (you may well say, 'After all that bother'), but the spathes will compensate for their scarcity by remaining colourful for two months or more. Even when cut and placed in water they will give anything from four to six weeks of pleasure.

A. scherzerianum is a much more suitable room plant, being very much easier to manage, and will do well where warmth, moist conditions and shelter from sunlight are provided. The flamingo plant, as it is commonly known, has red spathes borne on shorter stems and a more compact habit of growth, which makes it a sought-after plant for indoor decoration. There is also an important consideration here for the nurseryman: being of compact and generally tidy habit the plant is very much easier to handle when packing it for transit. (A surprising number of plants, however attractive they may seem in the greenhouse, will never be really popular because of the problems encountered when packing and handling generally.)

Commercially, almost all of this variety is raised from seed which will germinate if temperatures in the seventies are available. It is important to keep the heat constant for small plants to maintain growth in the early stages. A really open, spongy compost is essential when potting on this plant, something akin to a fifty-fifty mixture of J.I.P.2 or 3 and peat, and it will be all the better if the peat is nice and coarse. Pot the plant gently and at all costs avoid packing the compost too tightly around the roots. One consolation is that when using a peaty compost it is almost impossible to pack the mixture really hard. If rain water is available for watering this will be a distinct advantage over hard tap water.

Normally a two-year lapse is recommended between potting stages when dealing with the general run of house plants, but this may have to be an annual task when *A. scherzerianum* is grown in agreeable conditions where roots are produced freely. Root inspection of the plant once annually in the spring of the year will indicate whether or not potting on is required. Too frequent removal of the plant from its growing pot should be avoided as this treatment will only result in damage to the root system. Before removing plants it is important to ensure that the compost is well watered some time in advance.

From a small collection of these plants one may expect flowers almost throughout the year, though the blooms may be few and far between in winter. To get the best from the flowers it is usually necessary to employ some form of support to keep the flower stalk erect. This can be a slender cane to which the flower stalk is tied immediately under the spathe, or a piece of stiff wire with an open 'U' loop at the top in which the flower may rest. Cut the cane or wire to the correct length before inserting it in the compost, as the spathe may be damaged if the support is longer than the stalk itself.

APHELANDRA

Mexico and Brazil. 16 to 18°C. (60 to 65°F.). Difficult.

Although difficult to maintain indoors over the years, the aphelandra is a reasonably easy plant to care for from the time of purchase until the yellow bracts begin to blacken and die off, which will be anything from five to six months. We hear many glowing accounts of how one should be able to flower plants regularly over the years, but this is really just so much eye-wash. It is not an easy task to flower second- and third-year plants even in ideal greenhouse conditions.

However, compared to the average life of a bunch of flowers, even if the aphelandra plant should die off completely after six months this is reasonable value for money, and there is a great deal of pleasure to be had in trying to make the plant do what the man in the book said was not very easy. It really is quite incredible the number of times that I have emphasised in a talk to a gardening club how difficult it is to grow such and such a subject in the greenhouse only to discover that little Mr Brown in the front row has an embarrassment of them growing on almost every window-sill in his house!

Essential advice from the time of purchase: it is vitally important to ensure that the compost is kept moist all the time, as dryness at the roots results in limp and bedraggled leaves which have a marked tendency to detach themselves from the main stem very soon afterwards. The aphelandra is also a pretty avid feeder and will require fertilising from the word go indoors. On account of the densely matted roots a thin, weak fertiliser will do very little for this particular plant. Feed them more frequently, or increase the maker's recommended dosage, and the results will be much improved. Provision of a little humidity around the plant will improve its performance, as will a situation that is light and protected from the direct rays of the sun.

In the past there have been several aphelandras offered by the commercial grower as potentially good house plants, but *A. squarrosa louisae* and the improved variety *A. s.* Brockfeld have had few really serious competitors. In the popularity stakes the latter of these two appears to be winning the day, mainly on account of its much brighter and more attractive foliage. There is little to choose between the quality of flowers produced.

The house plant grower with an experimental turn of mind may well be able to grow on aphelandra plants from one year to the next if he has at his disposal some simple propagating equipment with which to raise new cuttings. To do this allow the bract to die back and lose its colour before cutting the plant back to a firm pair of leaves. Growth that appears from the axils of those leaves should be allowed to develop two pairs of leaves of their own before they are severed from the parent plant. A clean cut straight across the stem should be made about half an inch below the lower leaf. Propagate in a pure peat mixture and pot on into a proper growing compost as soon as the plant has rooted through to the sides of the small pot in which it has been propagated. From this second pot the plant will have to be potted on into at least one more pot size during that season provided the cuttings were struck early enough in

the year. Then, who knows, with a little luck you may have your very own aphelandra plants in flower by the end of the year.

ARALIA SIEBOLDII (FATSIA JAPONICA)

Japan. 7 to 18°C. (45 to 65°F.). Easy.

This plant seems to have survived quite happily with two names for many years, and in many parts of the country it appears to do equally well as a hardy garden shrub and as a house plant. In spite of being a comparatively cheap florist's plant it has always been a particular favourite of mine, one reason being that it does a great deal of work. In display terms such a plant is one that can be relied on to fill a reasonable section of the exhibition area with very little bother; being pleasantly green in colour it will fit with little difficulty into most colour schemes. It is also particularly useful as a bold individual plant where space can be afforded to show it off to full advantage. The wide temperature variation quoted above will give some indication of its toughness, but efforts should be made to acclimatise the plant to a reasonably even temperature, as wild fluctuations between 7 and 18°C. (45 and 65°F.) can be damaging no matter how tough it may be. When grown indoors *Aralia sieboldii* responds very well to standard treatment for the easier type of plant: moist compost, regular feeding and a light,

warm position. Red spider can be a bit bothersome in very dry atmospheric conditions, and soft new leaves attract greenfly; otherwise there are few problems. Propagation of new plants is simply done by means of seed.

There is also a variegated form that is something of a rarity and a little more difficult to manage, a slightly higher temperature being needed. Shortage of good stock is the main reason for the scarcity of this variety; as it is not possible to raise it from seed all propagation must be done vegetatively and shortage of stock plants puts a tight control on the number that can be produced in this way.

ARAUCARIA EXCELSA (Norfolk Island Pine)

Norfolk Island. 7 to 16°C. (45 to 60°F.). Easy.

In its native habitat a coniferous tree which will attain a height of 100 ft. or more, the Norfolk Island pine is, nevertheless, a plant that is superbly well equipped for cultivation as a house plant. Like the aralia mentioned previously it is a supremely elegant plant, producing tiers of well-spaced leaves of soft green colouring. It is capable of adjusting to a variety of temperatures but is really best suited to the cooler situation where the temperature ranges between 10 and 13°C. (50 and 55°F.). Good light is also important; other than that it simply requires 87 the standard treatment for easier indoor plants.

New plants can be raised by taking cuttings of the ends of young shoots raised in the usual way at a temperature of about 18°C. (65°F.). However, better balanced, more symmetrical plants are obtained from seed, a long, slow business, but plants so produced are usually worth the extra effort involved. Pot on into J.I.P.2 compost and grow on in good light, but avoid the possibility of leaf scorch to young leaves by protecting the plants from strong sunlight.

ARDISIA

15 to 21°C. (60 to 70°F.). Difficult.

For the plantsman desirous of obtaining a slow-growing house plant this one could possibly be the ultimate choice. The nurseryman may well sow the seed in the traditional manner in a reasonably high temperature in the spring of one year and find that he is on the board of directors by the time the plant has attained its maximum height of some 4 ft. and is ready to be marketed. Highly improbable, you may feel, but this has actually happened to my knowledge. Well-grown plants that have retained most of their foliage can be very attractive, the principal interest being the freely borne red berries. Being so lamentably slow in growth few mature plants are ever offered for sale but, if time is on your side, they are not difficult to raise from seed. Keep fairly warm and in good light; otherwise apply standard treatment in respect of water and fertiliser. Avoid the temptation of transferring small plants to too-large pots before they are ready, as this will only prove detrimental.

ASPARAGUS

South Africa. 10 to 18°C. (50 to 65°F.), 13 to 18°C. (55 to 65°F.). Easy and moderately easy.

Asparagus sprengeri is a supremely adaptable plant which can be planted in the garden-room border for the growth to climb wall or trellis or to provide graceful foliage spilling out of hanging baskets, or it can be used more conventionally as a pot plant. In any case, it will be little bother if given some sun protection and adequate moisture during the spring and summer months. It will also appreciate during the summer regular application of weak liquid fertiliser. New plants may be raised from seed sown in a reasonably high temperature, about 21°C. (70°F.), in the spring or, if only a few plants are needed, older clumps can be split up and the pieces planted individually. Do this

in spring, using a standard house plant compost.

The principal attraction of *Asparagus meyeri* is the compactness of the pale green foliage, which makes it an ideal plant for pot culture or for use in hanging baskets. Fronds achieve a maximum length of some 2 ft. and their neat, cylindrical shape is particularly attractive. Grow in light shade and keep warm and moist. Old clumps can be split up to make new plants in the early part of the year, or they may be raised from seed.

ASPIDISTRA LURIDA (Cast Iron Plant)

China. Minimum 13°C. (55°F.). Easy.

Earlier this century the aspidistra must have been an essential part of almost every parlour window, and there was many a young lad or lass who earned their Saturday pocket money by cleaning the leaves of Grandma's cast iron plant. This must indeed have been an unfor-

An odd characteristic of this plant is the way in which the rather insignificant mauve-coloured flowers are produced at soil level, not really seeming to be part of the plant itself.

ASPLENIUM NIDUS (Bird's Nest Fern)

South East Asia. 13 to 18°C. (55 to 65°F.). Moderately easy.

When well grown this plant must surely rate as one of the most beautiful of all foliage plants, with leaves of the palest green that grow in shuttlecock fashion from the centre of the pot, not at all like a fern in the conventional sense. New plants can be raised by sowing spores in sandy peat at almost any time, but this is a task best left to the professional as the amateur rarely has the sort of facilities required in order to succeed. However, young and mature plants are in steady supply for a keen market, so there is little need to raise one's own plants.

Water with tepid rain water for preference and endeavour to maintain a humid atmosphere – this is one reason for these plants being particularly suited to large bottle garden and glass-case cultivation. Also, like the aspidistra, the asplenium is very susceptible to leaf damage when cleaned with leaf-cleaning agents, and it is advisable to use only clear water and a soft sponge when removing dust from the leaves. Few pests are troublesome, but scale insects can be a nuisance; these are easily detected on the undersides of leaves and can be eradicated by wiping them off with gentle pressure using a soft sponge soaked in malathion solution.

ASTILBE

China and Japan. 10 to 16°C. (50 to 60°F.). Easy.

Often wrongly referred to as spiraea, the astilbes are useful for providing temporary colour in the garden room or indoors in early summer. While indoors it is absolutely essential that the compost is kept saturated at all times, and that the plant should enjoy a cool, light position. By itself the foliage has little to recommend it, so after flowering, plants should be planted out in the garden, preferably in a moist, shaded position. Adequate moisture at the roots is all important whether the plant is in a pot indoors, or planted outside.

When they have flowered indoors, the plants ought to be hardened off a little before being finally planted in the garden. New plants may be raised from seed or, more simply, by means of root division.

gettable introduction to house plants for many of them. The odd thing is that many of the modern chemicals used for cleaning can prove harmful to the otherwise very tolerant aspidistra, so have a care and test the product first before using it too freely on the entire plant.

The aspidistra is still reasonably popular but, because of its slow rate of growth, it is invariably costly and in short supply. As the common name suggests, it is very easy to manage and will tolerate a wide variety of conditions, though very hot sun should be avoided. Pot on into J.I.P.3 compost in March–April when it is absolutely necessary. In fact, with larger plants it is better to trim off part of the root ball and replant in the same pot with a little fresh compost in the bottom and top.

Water by immersing the pot in a bucket of water until all the air bubbles stop coming up, then allow to dry out before watering again. Permanently saturated compost should be avoided.

Aucuba japonica

AUCUBA JAPONICA (Spotted Laurel)

Japan. 7 to 13°C. (45 to 55°F.). Easy.

With so many more attractive indoor plants available it is not surprising that this evergreen shrub has lost much of its importance as a pot plant. Nevertheless, it is still useful in cool rooms and on terraces when planted in tubs. Propagate from seed, or from cuttings taken late in the year. The latter method presents little difficulty and is probably the best for anyone wishing to raise a few plants for personal use. Use John Innes compost when potting, as this is reasonably heavy and will tend to produce sturdier, more compact plants. When these become untidy and less attractive as pot plants they may be planted out in almost any position in the garden.

AZALEA INDICA

China. 7 to 13°C. (45 to 55°F.). Easy.

Of the flowering pot plants this is undoubtedly one of the most important and, in spite of the ever-increasing price, one cannot imagine that azaleas will fall off in popularity. Almost all the better quality plants available in Europe originate from Belgium where, it seems, there are areas particularly suited to the culture of *Azalea indica*. Available in a wide range of colours from white to deep red, they present little difficulty for the house plant grower who can provide the conditions they prefer. Initially, one should purchase plants with full foliage and plenty of flower buds with a small number of buds fully open. Don't be misled into believing that plants in very tight bud will give a longer flowering period – in some conditions they may not flower at all. The temperature advised above is that for maintaining plants in the best possible condition while they are indoors; plants will naturally have to endure higher temperatures when they are put out of doors during the summer months.

An adequate supply of water is the all-important consideration, as it will be totally fatal for the compost to dry out for any length of time. Soft water or rain water will invariably give better results. (In hard-water areas softer water can be provided simply by immersing a hessian sack filled with peat in a water butt or tub). Almost everyone has their pet way of watering pot plants, and there is no shortage of advice concerning the various methods to employ. But, with this plant, it is simply a question of keeping the compost wet, and this is best done by plunging the pot in a bucket of water daily and allowing all the air bubbles to emerge before withdrawing it. To prolong the flowering period of the plant indoors it is essential that it should be kept in a cool room, as hot, dry conditions will accelerate flower and bud development. Good light is also necessary.

In order to carry plants over from one year to the next it is important that they should not be neglected during the summer months. Flowers should be removed as they fade, taking care not to damage any new growth that may be sprouting under them. Keep the plant moist and in a light, cool room indoors until all chance of frost has gone. It may then be placed out of doors until such time as the weather changes when it should be brought in again. In order to reduce the necessity for watering, plants should enjoy a light, cool position in the garden. A shallow trench can be dug and filled with moist peat into which the plant pots are plunged to their rims, or, if you are not particularly keen on digging trenches, plant pots can be placed on a firm stone or concrete base and moist peat can be banked up around them. While out of doors the foliage should be sprayed over regularly and the compost kept moist. When potting on becomes necessary a very open, lime-free compost incorporating a substantial amount of good leaf-mould is required.

When the plants are brought in from the garden the cool, light room is again the ideal place until such time as flower buds are just visible; the temperature is then increased until flowers have begun to open. Thereafter the temperature should be maintained in the region of 10°C. (50°F.) in order to prolong the flowering time for as long as possible. In the first year after purchase the amount of flower may be disappointing, but this is usually rectified in subsequent years. As the years go by plants will lose the symmetrical and neat shape they had at the time of purchase. Careful pruning will put this right, but many of the following year's flowers will be forfeited as a result, so it is often wise to leave well alone.

BAMBUSA (Bamboo)

South East Asia. Minimum 7°C. (45°F.). Easy.

Tall, elegant grasses, bamboos are ideal where ample space can be provided for them to develop naturally. The high and spacious room is best, where plants can be placed as individual features, or they are ideally suited for planting around indoor pools in more elaborate planting features. They will also do well if planted out in the border of the garden room as a background to other more colourful plants.

When potting, a heavier compost such as J.I.P.3 should be used, and the potting should be done fairly firmly. New plants may be raised from seed sown in good heat, preferably in the spring, from cuttings of rhizomes done at the same time of the year or, often more simple, by division of the roots in the early part of the year so that plants have an opportunity to become established over the summer months. Keep the compost moist during the spring and summer months and less so in winter.

BEAUCARNEA RECURVATA (NOLINA TUBERCULATA) (Ponytail Plant)

Mexico. 10 to 18°C. (50 to 65°F.). Easy.

Grown from seed, the ponytail plant has narrow recurving green leaves that radiate from a central bulb not unlike a somewhat coarse onion in appearance, and is a most attractive plant that deserves to be better known than at present. Essentially an individual plant on account of its symmetrical form, it requires a lightly shaded position and moderate watering. To retain the attractive compact appearance it is advisable

Apricot Beauty, a fibrous-rooted begonia

to use J.I.P.3 compost and to pot fairly firmly. In order to retain a proper balance between pot and plant the new pot should not be excessively large.

BEGONIA

13 to 18°C. (55 to 65°F.). Moderately easy.

For such a colourful and diverse family of plants it would be impossible to give a country of origin. The temperature given above is merely offered as a general guide and, on the whole, they are moderately easy.

Begonia rex is probably the most familiar as far as pot plants go, and these are offered by nurserymen the world over in a wide range of exciting colours. Reasonably good light is required and a temperature of not less than 16°C. (60°F.) should be the aim. The majority of pot plants will last for at least one year after purchase before they need potting on into larger containers. However, it is my experience that *B. rex* quickly deteriorates once it has become pot bound, so instead of waiting for the 91 customary year, it is better to transfer plants to larger pots almost immediately on purchase provided it is not in the middle of the winter. New pots should be only a little larger and the compost needs to be open, something akin to two parts J.I.P.3 and one part fresh sphagnum peat. In time it is almost inevitable that plants will become mis-shapen in appearance; it may then be a good time to experiment in producing new plants as described in the chapter on propagation. In close conditions *B. rex* is susceptible to mildew attack; this is best controlled by Benlate powder applied as required.

Fibrous-rooted begonias are among the most interesting of foliage pot plants, many of them producing a quite spectacular amount of colourful flowers throughout the spring and summer months. The majority being reasonably easy to care for, it is hard to understand why they should not be much more popular than they are at present. The owner of the lightly shaded and reasonably warm garden room or greenhouse who wishes to specialise in something different may well consider these plants. For taller growing plants (4 to 6 ft.) a choice could be made from *B. fuchsioides*, *B. lucerna*, *B. haageana* or *B. maculata*. For hanging baskets there can be few better than *B. glaucophylla*, which has pale green leaves that contrast well with the darker mature leaves. The principal attraction, however, is the mass of pendulous flowers that appear early in the year; these may be anything from rose pink to brick red in colour, depending to some extent on the conditions in which they are grown.

There are many smaller and more compact varieties which do well as indoor plants and one has only to send to a specialist nursery for a list in order to make a selection. All will do well in a temperature in the region of 16°C. (60°F.), and require more or less standard house plant treatment. When plants become old and leggy, as they do in time, new plants may be raised from cuttings which will root fairly readily in close, warm conditions.

Selected seed from the tuberous-rooted species produce some of the most spectacular flowers of all pot plants, or you can purchase the tubers and get results in a much shorter space of time. Not difficult to grow, the tubers are started in boxes of peat in mid-February and potted on into 5-in. pots when they have produced a cluster of new leaves. Thereafter it is a question of keeping them well fed, moist and at a temperature in the region of 13 to 16°C. (55 to 60°F.). In the autumn when plants die down naturally the tubers should be dried and stored in a warm place until the following February. The tuberous-rooted pendulous varieties can

also be most impressive when planted in hanging baskets, as great panicles of flower hang down, almost obliterating the baskets. Needless to say, there is an almost infinite range of colours, and, generally speaking, the more you pay for the tubers or seed the better the plants and flowers will be.

It is not often that a new plant is readily accepted by nurseryman, florist and general public, but this would indeed seem to be the case with *Begonia* Fireglow. Unfortunately it masquerades under a variety of names at the time of writing. Of compact appearance, it has bright green leaves (an advantage in any plant) and flowers that have an almost fluorescent orange appearance. Most important of all is the fact that it is a particularly good indoor plant, requiring a light, warm location and compost which is kept moist but never saturated for long periods or too dry. Keep the plants on the move by regular applications of liquid fertiliser, as they seem more susceptible to fungus troubles when they are growing less well. Treat mildew with Benlate powder fungicide. After flowering the old flower stalks should be removed, and at the same time the plant can be gently pruned to a better shape. When resting in the winter keep the compost a little dryer and refrain from feeding. One can get really enthusiastic about this variety and say that it is a pot plant with a considerable future.

Finally, there is *B. masoniana*, which is grown in sufficient quantities to be considered as a plant apart from the general run of begonias. Most plants get their common names for descriptive reasons and this one is no exception – the name iron cross is given because of the distinctive brown iron cross marking in the centre of each leaf. It is a supremely useful display plant which seems to fit in with almost any colour scheme, whether it be in a small planted bowl or in a major flower show exhibit. The treatment is almost exactly that described for *B. rex*, except that it is not quite so prone to mildew attack.

BELOPERONE (Shrimp Plant)

South America. 10 to 16°C. (50 to 60°F.). Easy.

Beloperone guttata is the best known species and gets its common name again for a descriptive reason, this time because the flowering bracts bear a distinct resemblance to small shrimps – or large shrimps, depending on how well the plants have been grown! This is another plant that must be kept on the move if it is to do well, as any neglect in the way of feeding, or too long   93 a delay in potting on, will surely result in the plant becoming hard and lacking in lustre. Plants can be raised from cuttings; we are usually advised to insert one cutting in a small pot, but better results will be obtained if four or five cuttings are inserted around the edge of the pot. A convenient way of raising them is to fill the pot with J.I.P.2 compost, make holes for the cuttings with a pencil and fill the holes with moist peat. The cuttings are then inserted in the peat in which they will root before finding their way into the compost, where they will grow very much better.

One snag with these plants is that they will very often flower so freely in the early stages that they will almost kill themselves off, as all the energy goes into producing coloured bracts and very little is directed to the production of new leaves. Therefore, it is wise at the beginning to be a bit harsh and remove all the early bracts as they appear, so building up a much more

healthy and robust plant. Also, in the early stages it is advisable occasionally to remove the growing tips of new shoots in order to induce a more bushy and compact habit of growth. Once the plant has begun to grow with reasonable freedom it will be essential to ensure that a regular programme of feeding with a balanced liquid fertiliser is started and maintained until the plant is potted on. This is an operation that should be performed at least once annually. Robust plants may be potted more often, and in a couple of years you may have plants from cuttings as much as 4 ft. in height and bracts which are 6 in. or more in length. Not possible, according to most books on the subject, but it is quite possible in good conditions if one is prepared to remove all the bracts as they appear for the first twelve months or so.

Beloperone lutea is an interesting and colourful plant with greenish-yellow bracts which can provide an exciting display on older specimens.

Beloperone guttata

Actually this plant is never at its best until it has been potted into a pot 7 in. or more in size. It can then be a most impressive sight when massed around green-leaved plants such as monsteras. This variety is still very much in short supply, but should you be fortunate enough to obtain one the treatment is much the same as that advised for *guttata*.

BILLBERGIA NUTANS

Brazil. 10 to 16°C. (50 to 60°F.). Easy.

Of all the many bromeliads this is one of the easiest to grow, and will acclimatise to a wide temperature range, though it is better if plants can be grown within the limits advised above. Flowering bracts are short lived and interesting in shape, but not particularly exciting as bromeliads go. New plants are easily propagated from offshoots, and these grow at a fairly prodigious rate, so plants will need to be potted on at least once every second year. They are quite useful in small hanging baskets where the pendulous bracts will be seen to good effect and the plants can grow into reasonably sized clumps without getting in the way.

Billbergia windii is almost identical, but not quite such a vigorous grower compared to *nutans*. Its main distinguishing feature is its broader leaves. Care and attention is no different.

BROMELIADS

South America. 13 to 16°C. (55 to 60°F.). Easy.

This is another section of plants which may well appeal to anyone wishing to specialise. Almost all of them have overlapping leaves rising like a large rosette from the centre of the growing pot. These make a perfectly watertight urn that must

Billbergia windii

at all times be kept filled with water. With the vast majority the compost in the pot should be kept only just moist, as the root systems are not especially strong and are easily damaged by continual saturation.

Many of the bromeliads are epiphytes which in their native habitat attach themselves to tree branches and old logs and make their home there. The process is frequently started by birds depositing seed in the bark of the tree where it will germinate and flourish in spite of the meagre foothold.

For a novel effect in the garden room or greenhouse it can be a lot of fun to make a bromeliad tree. This is done by acquiring an interestingly shaped, fairly firm tree branch and anchoring it in a large pot filled with concrete. Once the concrete sets there will be a firm anchorage for plants and the arrangement will be reasonably portable. For this purpose the smaller bromeliads are the most suitable, tillandsias and cryptanthus in particular. Plants should be knocked out of their pots and the soil ball should be wrapped in wet sphagnum moss. The plant is then fixed to the tree branch as unobtrusively as possible with plastic-covered wire. Thereafter the moss should be kept permanently moist. It will be found that many of the plants will do very much better and will certainly be much more interesting when treated in this way.

Most of the bromeliads may be propagated with little difficulty from young plants which develop at the base of the parent stem. They can also be raised from fresh seed with reasonable ease; in fact, should one be foolish enough to save all the seed that may be produced by one plant of *Aechmea bracteata* and raise them successfully there would in time be enough plants to fill almost every room in the house – from floor to ceiling!

Knowing that the majority of the more interesting bromeliads are in short supply it would be foolish to provide here a lengthy list of plants which would, in all probability, be unobtainable. There are, however, specialist nurseries which issue lists of available plants, and this is by far the best way of setting out to acquire a collection. There are also a number of societies catering especially for the bromeliad, from whom a great deal of information may be obtained concerning the supply of plants.

Some of the more important members of the bromeliad family are also dealt with separately here in alphabetical order under the name of the appropriate genus. For aechmea see page 76, ananas page 81, billbergia page 94, cryptanthus page 113, neoregelia page 149, tillandsia page 181, and vriesia page 183.

96

BOUGAINVILLEA (Paper Flower)

Brazil. October to February 10 to 13°C. (50 to 55°F.), March to September 16°C. (60°F.) and above. Easy.

The 'easy' tag must apply only to plants grown in the garden room or greenhouse, as the light conditions available indoors would present problems. In the light garden room they can be most impressive when in full colour; to achieve this it is important that plants should be kept very much on the dry side during the winter months when they are resting. When new growth is evident, usually in February, the amount of water should be gradually increased and thereafter the compost should be kept moist but never permanently saturated until the plants begin to shed their leaves naturally towards the end of the summer.

Richly coloured bracts will give a much more effective show if growth is trained to a trellis or wire support in the shape of a fan. Plants should be hard pruned in February, the previous year's growth being cut back to an inch or two in length. Good light is all important as results are invariably poor in shaded conditions. Pests are not too troublesome, though mealy bug can be a problem, particularly when growth becomes matted and there is difficulty in making contact with the bugs when spraying.

Increase by means of cuttings about 3 to 5 in. in length and taken with a heel, inserting them in a warm propagating frame. In good rooting conditions it is surprising how well some of the toughest old pieces will produce roots.

BRUNFELSIA CALYCINA

Brazil. October to March minimum 10°C. (50°F.), April to September 16 to 19°C. (60 to 65°F.). Difficult.

Only occasionally available, there are several varieties of brunfelsia in shades that range from white through lavender to purple, but *Brunfelsia calycina* is the most frequently met with. This grows to about 2 ft. in height and flowers in summer, at which time the compost should be kept fairly moist, and the plant will benefit if the foliage is sprayed over regularly with a fine spray. Also, feeding should not be neglected in summer as foliage quickly takes on a sickly yellow appearance. Any potting on that is needed should be done in late summer after flowering, using J.I.P.2 or 3. Pot firmly and ensure that the pots are adequately drained. Propagate from cuttings about 4 in. in length taken in the spring; a warm propagator will be necessary for housing the cuttings.

CALADIUM

Brazil. 16 to 22°C. (60 to 71°F.). Difficult.

These tuberous-rooted members of the aroid family are started into growth in February when the temperature should be maintained at the maximum 22°C. (71°F.) advised above. Tubers will, however, start into growth more rapidly if the temperature can be kept a little above this level. For preference they should be started in boxes or beds of moist peat in a heated greenhouse where they will soon get under way and can be potted into a standard house plant compost some four to six weeks later. If stock is to be increased the tubers can first be divided, care being taken to dust the cut areas with charcoal to reduce the possibility of rotting. Keep the plants in the warmer greenhouse area until they have produced several leaves, then gradually acclimatise them to lower temperatures in the region of 16°C. (60°F.).

These are among the most attractive of foliage plants and will considerably enhance any collection, but it is important that they should enjoy adequate temperatures, as they are invariably poor and miserable in cooler conditions. Only specialised nurseries will list them and there are varieties in many exotic colours, but the *candidum* variety with its green-veined, white leaves must surely lead the field. It is also one of the most durable; even so one should not expect more than about four months' pleasure from the plant before it begins to deteriorate and die back naturally for the winter.

At this stage the amount of water given should be reduced until the compost is quite dry. The plant should be kept in this dry condition from the time it has lost all its leaves until the

Calathea picturata

growing process begins again in February. It must be emphasised, however, that it is not easy to keep plants from one year to the next unless the tubers can be kept in warm and agreeable conditions. Keep them moist when in active growth, but allow the compost to dry a little between each watering, otherwise roots are likely to be damaged by overwet compost.

CALATHEA

Tropical America. 19 to 25°C. (65 to 75°F.). Difficult.

These supremely beautiful plants are not for the beginner. Many of them will test the skill of the most accomplished expert, and should he succeed the amateur grower may well feel he has advanced some way towards earning the enviable title of 'greenfingers'. There are many varieties to choose from, but they are not often available in other than limited quantities, though they are worth the bother of hunting out if you feel that you can provide the necessary conditions. Warmth is essential and a temperature of not less than 19°C. (65°F.) should be the aim. And the need for a moist atmosphere and shaded situation cannot be over emphasised. Even with these conditions it will be difficult to stop the tips and edges of many varieties becoming brown in time. Much of this condition is brought on by compost that lies cold and wet for long periods. An open, peaty compost that drains freely is recommended, so it is important that the pots should have ample drainage. Clay pots are best as the compost drains more freely in them, and clay pots give better results with plants that are likely to be in the same pot for any length of time.

Calatheas are often seen growing at their best when planted in warm borders in agreeably heated greenhouses or garden rooms. Growth freely produced in this way is ideal material from which to increase stock. When fairly large clumps have been produced they can be dug up and divided into smaller clumps and either potted or planted out to grow on.

Calathea insignis is a striking plant with long, narrow leaves which are coloured dull purple on the reverse side and have pale green upper surfaces with contrasting darker green markings. For the flower arranger the cut leaves have a natural stiffness that can be particularly exciting as the dominant feature in an arrangement.

Calathea ornata has longer petioles and more rounded leaves, but is, if anything, more exotically marked than *insignis* – it is also a little more difficult to care for. *C. picturata* is similar in shape with slightly shorter leaf stalks, but has quite different colouring; the entire centre of the leaf is silver grey in appearance with a dark green margin, the reverse being dull red and a complete contrast. *C. louisae* is usually more easily obtained and is slightly easier to care for than most; leaves are of medium green colouring and have irregular mottled variegation around the centre rib.

Calathea makoyana is frequently sold as *Maranta makoyana*, and has the common name of peacock plant. The common name is not inappropriate, as this must surely rate as one of the most attractive plant leaves. It seems incredible that so much colour can be incorporated in a leaf that is so thin it would almost seem to be transparent. Under normal conditions the growth attains a height of little more than 15 to 18 in., but some specialists can get them up to about 4 ft. from the base of the pot. This sort of achievement would, one suspects, be far beyond the ability of the amateur with less sophisticated facilities.

CALCEOLARIA (Slipper Flower)

South America. 13°C. (55°F.). Easy.

Although plants may easily be raised from seed by following the directions on the seed packet, it is usually better for the indoor gardener to purchase a few plants as required. Bought as young plants, calceolarias may easily be grown on by potting into larger containers as required, using J.I.P.2 or 3 compost, depending on the size of the pot. On the whole, they are comparatively easy plants to care for if given a light and reasonably cool position in which to grow. Aphids are the most troublesome pests, also whitefly, so one should keep a watchful eye for them and treat before they get too much of a hold. Once established in their final pots much better results will be had if the plants are fed regularly with a good fertiliser used a little stronger than the manufacturer suggests. Plants should be disposed of after they have flowered and are past their best.

CALLISTEMON (Bottle Brush)

Australia. Minimum 7 to 10°C. (45 to 50°F.). Easy.

These are amusing shrubs that will do well in the garden for a temporary period during the more settled months of the year, and make grand plants when grown in tubs on the terrace or in the garden room. They will also do very well if planted out in the border of the garden room to give a much bolder effect. The principal interest

99

Opposite: On the shelf, from left to right, are *Dracaena terminalis, Aphelandra squarrosa* Brockfeld, *Dracaena sanderiana* (behind), *Ficus pumila, Dracaena* Rededge, and *Dracaena godseffiana* Florida Beauty. In the foreground, also from left to right, are *Ficus radicans variegata, Dieffenbachia arvida exotica, Begonia rex* and *Pilea* Moon Valley

is in their scarlet to orange flower spikes that resemble bottle or flue brushes. Comparatively easy to grow, they prefer a reasonably heavy compost similar to J.I.P.3 and free drainage. Some of the pot-grown varieties are now being treated with growth-restricting chemicals which keep plants much more compact and which, as is often the case with these chemicals, induce them to produce many more flowers than they would if left to grow naturally.

To increase stock, cuttings should be taken about 4 in. in length from young wood; they will root more easily if taken with a heel, a piece of the older wood of the plant still attached to the cutting. Plants may also be raised from seed. *C. citrinus* is the one that is most often offered for sale as a pot plant. Fortunately it is comparatively free of pests.

CAMELLIA

China, Japan. September to March 4 to 10°C. (40 to 50°F.), April to August 13 to 16°C. (55 to 60°F.). Moderately easy.

Camellias are good pot plants, and particularly good plants for the cool greenhouse or garden room where they can be planted out in the border to give a wonderful display. Naturally glossy foliage is in itself attractive and, added to this,

there is the pleasure of beautifully cool, single and double flowers in a wide range of colours. Lime-free soil is an essential requirement and it is also important to ensure that plants are watered with rain, or lime-free water. Pruning should be minimal, and only untidy shoots should be trimmed to shape in the spring of the year. Loss of buds by dropping prematurely can be a problem; this is usually caused by very dry conditions at the roots or by excessive fluctuations in temperature, particularly if it becomes too cold.

CAMPANULA ISOPHYLLA (Star of Bethlehem)

Italy. Minimum 4°C. (40°F.). Moderately easy.

Because of the amount of work involved in tying in foliage these are shunned by many nurserymen, but this is because of the tendency to grow them as upright plants. They are, in fact, the most superb hanging basket plants that one could possibly wish for – a height of between 4 and 8 in. is frequently quoted as a maximum, but when grown in baskets they may extend to 3 ft. or more. *C. isophylla* is blue; *C. i. mayii* is mauve and *C. i. alba* is white and by far the best of the three, especially as a trailing plant.

Callistemon, the bottle-brush plant

Plants are raised from spring-struck cuttings, several inserted in each small pot to give a full effect. When established in their pots three or four plants should be placed in each basket, using J.I.P.3 compost. Water plants in, then keep them on the dry side until they have got under way. From then on it is absolutely essential that they do not dry out; active plants will require a good two to three pints of water daily. Drying out will result in shrivelling of the leaves and complete ruination of the plant. Smaller plants may be grown in pots fixed in wall brackets, but they need much more attention.

The flowering period is usually from July through to the end of September. After flowering, plants lose their appearance and should be cut hard back and kept in dryer condition. They can then be overwintered in temperatures as low as the 4°C. (40°F.) mentioned above.

Another nice feature is that, provided they are kept well watered and fed regularly while in active growth, they seem able to tolerate the most incredible fluctuations in temperature. Any owner of a small greenhouse or garden room will appreciate that this is quite an asset, as plants are often exposed unavoidably to very wide variations in temperature in small glassed-in areas which are impossible to ventilate adequately.

CAREX MORROWII VARIEGATA

Japan. 13 to 16°C. (55 to 60°F.). Easy.

This sedge does best in the temperatures advised, but will tolerate wide variations and is quite hardy in milder areas. Frequently sold under the name *Carex japonica*, it is an ideal choice for planting around the edge of the small indoor or garden-room pool; this also gives a clue to the fact that it must be kept moist at all times. It is also an extremely useful plant for incorporating

Carex morrowii variegata

in small mixed plantings in decorative bowls, the pleasant cream-and-green striped grass giving a pleasing change of shape.

Plants can be increased by means of seed sown in the spring, or if only a few plants are needed they can be obtained very easily by dividing the grassy clumps at almost any time of the year. These are good plants for the beginner to experiment with as they seem pest and trouble free.

CERASTIUM TOMENTOSUM (Snow in Summer)

Europe. 4 to 10°C. (40 to 50°F.). Easy.

The reader in all probability feels that, in suggesting this plant, the writer has taken leave of his senses, as it is normally associated with being a particularly invasive garden plant – almost a weed, in fact. So why include it here? Recently on a visit to a famous parks department nursery in the South of England my attention was arrested by a very unusual and attractive plant in a hanging basket: it was a complete and beautiful ball of silver. You've guessed, it was snow in summer, growing as I had never seen it before. The parks manager informed me that they did numerous experiments of this kind, and the cerastium was one that had paid off handsomely. By putting a dozen or so cuttings directly into a hanging basket containing J.I.P.3 compost you could not wish for anything less expensive, and you may well surprise your acquaintances as they look at your creation, not daring to suggest that it can possibly be that awful plant that creeps into the garden from the neighbour's patch next door.

CEROPEGIA WOODII (Hearts Entangled)

South Africa. September to March 4 to 10°C. (40 to 50°F.), April to August 13 to 16°C. (55 to 60°F.). Easy.

Interesting rather than decorative, these plants have masses of fleshy, heart-shaped leaves on thread-like growth that resemble small hearts entwined around one another; hence the common name. Colouring is predominantly grey speckled with green. Propagation is effected by means of fragile young cuttings taken at almost any time of the year, although spring is best, or plants may be allowed to run over a bed of peat into which they will root quite freely; it is then a simple question of snipping off the rooted pieces and potting them up individually. Give them a light position and avoid overwatering; plants are set off to best advantage when trailing from small hanging baskets or pots placed in wall brackets. Keep in small pots as long as possible, and when potting on use any good house plant mixture.

CESTRUM ELEGANS

Mexico. September to March 4 to 10°C. (40 to 50°F.), March to September 13 to 16°C. (55 to 60°F.). Easy.

An old-fashioned greenhouse climbing plant that has, in recent years, been struggling to make the grade as a viably commercial pot plant. Dull green foliage reduces its chance of success, but there is some compensation in the abundance of wine-red, pendulous flowers which are produced over a long period during the summer months. However, it is much more of a garden-room plant than a house plant, as growth is generally better and more effective when the

Cestrum elegans

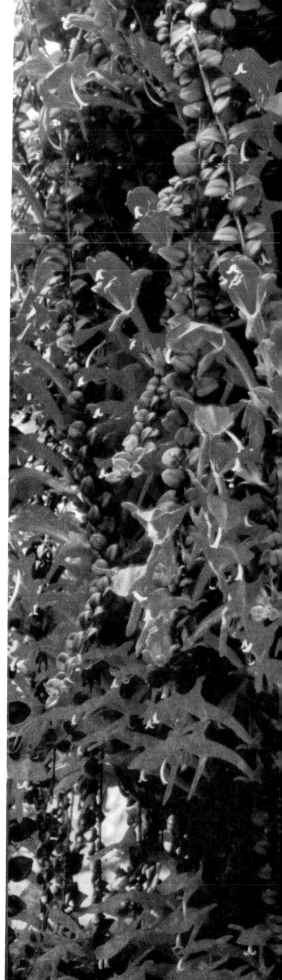

Almost the perfect plant for a hanging basket, *Columnea gloriosa* provides a dramatic cascade of colour. Columneas are not hard to grow if given sufficient warmth and moisture

plant is fanned out against a wall and in time allowed to grow along the underside of the roof; flowers can then be seen to much better advantage. Pot in fairly large pots using J.I.P.3 compost, or plant freely in the garden-room border in the same mixture. Prune back fairly hard after flowering and keep on the dry side during the winter months. Cuttings prepared from the pruned growth will root with little difficulty.

CHLOROPHYTUM COMOSUM (Spider Plant)

South Africa. Minimum 7°C. (45°F.). Easy.

Everybody's favourite, this plant can often be seen growing in the most appalling conditions and must surely rate as one of the most durable of all house plants. There can be few schools and offices about the country that do not have their sprinkling of chlorophytums dotted around the window-sills. It seems pointless to stipulate temperatures for this plant, as it seems to do perfectly well in temperatures of the widest variation, but somewhere in the region of 13°C. (55°F.) should be aimed at as ideal. In this temperature plants will retain their fresh, crisp appearance, which they often lose in too-hot conditions, or when the compost is kept excessively wet for long periods.

Whenever these plants are mentioned among a group of people the question of leaf tips turning brown will invariably crop up. All sorts of answers are put forward and remedies suggested, but to my mind chlorophytum leaf tips turn brown simply because of starvation. As they increase in size the plants develop an astonishing number of thick, fleshy roots which wind around in the bottom of the pot and, having nothing to feed on, the paucity of nourishment is reflected in the brown leaf condition. Regular feeding will help, but frequent potting on is the only real answer. However, this will result in having to use pots of quite large proportion in a short space of time, so it is often better to snip off brown leaf tips. Alternatively the leaves can be removed completely and no harm will be done as there is always a plentiful supply of new leaves if plants are healthy.

In time the plants will produce long, arching stems at the end of which new plantlets will form. These root very easily if pegged down into fresh compost, and are detached from the parent plant when they have developed roots.

In spite of being everyday plants chlorophytums are excellent value and ideal for planting in front of prepared beds indoors, or for incorporating in container arrangements in offices and larger rooms.

104

CHRYSANTHEMUM

Japan. 13 to 19°C. (55 to 65°F.). Easy.

The compact florist's chrysanthemum of recent years needs little introduction here, mainly on account of its universal popularity and its ease of cultivation. In the greenhouse plants are raised from cuttings, five to each 5-in. pot, treated with a growth depressant chemical and given controlled light conditions in order to induce them to flower when required rather than when they would tend to flower naturally. These plants flower according to the length of the day and the amount of light that is available, so by using black polythene to simulate shorter day conditions the plants can be persuaded to flower at any time of the year. On average, this is about ten weeks after insertion of the cuttings.

Under natural conditions the potted plants would grow to normal chrysanthemum height, but by use of carefully measured doses of chemical plants can be restricted to a maximum growing height of some 18 in., which makes them a much more marketable proposition as decorative flowering plants. Indoors, plants can almost be guaranteed to last for eight to ten weeks from the time of purchase, needing little more attention than regular watering and a light, warm room in which to grow.

Following their spell indoors they can be planted out in the garden where they will grow to normal chrysanthemum height once they cease to be affected by the growth-retarding chemical. Unfortunately these chemicals are rarely available outside the trade, so one must be satisfied with taller plants once they have been planted out.

CISSUS ANTARCTICA (Kangaroo Vine)

Australia. Minimum 10°C. (50°F.), maximum 19°C. (65°F.). Easy.

A vigorous climbing plant with rich, glossy green leaves that does best in temperatures in the region of 16°C. (60°F.). In higher temperatures there is a marked tendency for leaves to turn brown and eventually drop off. In spite of this drawback it is still one of the most popular of house plants, needing relatively average conditions in order to succeed, a cool, lightly shaded situation being best. Potting on is required every second year, but once plants have reached 10-in. pots they can usually be sustained simply by regular feeding. Grown as climbers fanned out on a trellis form of support, they provide an excellent background for other plants, or they can be equally effective grown without supports as ground cover in larger beds

or troughs which contain a collection of plants.

They are very easily propagated from easily rooted cuttings, but they should be potted up with at least four cuttings to each pot in order to provide bushier plants.

CITRUS MITIS (Calamondin Orange)

America. Half hardy. Moderately easy.

When anything goes wrong with a citrus plant then the florist, nurseryman and everyone down the line is in trouble. The main reason is that these are expensive plants to buy and the purchaser is more likely as a consequence to seek advice. When first bought, plants normally have an abundance of glossy green leaves, small orange-coloured fruits, green unripened fruit and, for good measure, heavily scented white flowers. With all these attractions the plant is almost bound to be costly, even if you discount the length of time it takes to bring it to maturity: the longer plants spend in the heated greenhouses of the nursery the more the customer will have to pay for them.

The principal reason for plants failing to do well indoors is inadequate watering, and is certainly the reason for leaves curling and losing their colour before eventually dropping off. The majority of nurserymen go to a great deal of trouble in printing name labels and advice tickets but it is extremely difficult to convey by the printed word what is required of the purchaser, who often knows nothing at all about plants. It is also difficult to prescribe exact amounts of water as almost all plants are varied in their requirements, and the nurseryman has no knowledge of the sort of environment into which the plants will be introduced. My advice is to give a really good watering and to allow the compost to dry out a little before watering again. Do this by plunging the plant pot in a bucketful of tepid water and allow all the air in the pot to escape before withdrawing it. This will ensure that water soaks right through to the bottom of the pot, which is important. For a large, well-rooted plant such as the citrus it is not much good pouring a pint or so of water onto the top of the pot as this is only likely to penetrate the top soil while the bulk of the root system remains dry, so make a thorough job of it. Feed only when the plant is producing new leaves, and use a weak liquid fertiliser frequently rather than give occasional heavy doses.

The best of these miniature oranges are produced in the southern states of America and from there they are shipped to many countries around the world to be grown on before being resold. So when purchasing these plants it is important to remember that they come originally from a very sunny climate and it will be wise to expose them to as much sunshine as possible. This will entail putting them out into a sheltered, sunny spot in the garden during the summer months of the year. The only pruning necessary is light trimming of longer shoots. Cuttings made from these trimmings will not be difficult to root in warm, close conditions, but they will take a long time to make plants of any size. Given good heat and moist conditions it is also reasonably easy to germinate seed. The fruits are about the size of small tangerine oranges, but rather bitter tasting – if you have sufficient oranges to spare they do make excellent marmalade. To give some idea of the amount of fruit that is possible on one plant, one recent writer claimed that his *C. mitis* had over two hundred oranges on the branches, a spectacular result considering that it was the plant's third year in a living-room window position.

Scale insects can be a messy and troublesome pest on this plant, so keep a watchful eye for their presence, particularly along the main stem.

Besides the dwarf *C. mitis* there are many other members of the citrus family that one can experiment with, but it should be borne in mind that these may take up to ten years to produce fruits, whereas *C. mitis* will oblige in three to four years.

CLERODENDRUM THOMSONAE

Tropical Africa. 13 to 19°C. (55 to 65°F.). Moderately easy.

A climbing shrub which can produce the most spectacular amount of flower during the summer months. The white flowers with crimson centres are produced in large clusters on individual stems all the way up the plant from the base of the stem to the uppermost branches. If kept on the dry side the plants may be grown at lower temperatures than that specified above, but foliage takes on a harder appearance and they are generally less attractive.

Clerodendrums are excellent subjects for fanning out against a wall, or they may be used as a central feature if placed in 10-in. pots or in tubs. If the latter method is chosen it is wise to push four or five 6-ft. canes into the compost close to the edge of the pot, pulling the canes together at the top and tying them securely. Growth can then be wound around these supports and a much more impressive plant will result.

Plants will require ample moisture and feeding from March through to September, with moderate watering until about the beginning of November when they will have shed most of their leaves. Thereafter they will remain dormant until early March and can be kept quite dry, but it is important that they should enjoy warm winter quarters. As new growth appears the watering process should be gradually restarted, care being taken not to have the compost too wet before plants have developed a reasonable amount of fresh foliage.

Unless long growth is needed for filling in gaps one should prune the new season's growths back to about 3 or 4 in. from their base immediately after plants have flowered. These trimmings are usually rough and scraggy, so of little use for propagation purposes. To increase plants it is much better to make cuttings a few inches in length from the first growth that is produced in the spring. These cuttings will need very warm temperatures, however, something in excess of 22°C. (72°F.) if they are to have a chance of success.

CLIANTHUS

Australia, New Zealand. Minimum 16°C. (60°F.). Difficult.

Not a plant for the beginner, but a most rewarding exotic plant for the person who can provide the correct conditions and the extra bit of care that is wanted. To mention a few of the common names will give an indication of how exotic it is: glory pea, parrot's bill, red kowhai and lobster's claw. Again, they are multi-purpose plants which may be planted in the border in the garden room, grown in pots, or used in hanging baskets, where they are even more impressive as one can see the exciting flowers much better than when they are in pots or against a wall.

Plants may be raised from seed sown in warm conditions, or from cuttings of side shoots inserted in a warm propagator at a temperature of not less than 22°C. (72°F.). *Clianthus dampieri*, the glory pea, requires special treatment and is very much a task for the experienced professional; having weak roots it must be grafted on to seedling stock of *Colutea arborescens*. When purchasing this plant it is probably much better to enquire about plants that have already been grafted and established on the new stock.

Most careful watering is necessary from October to March and during the remainder of the year it is important to ensure that the compost is not allowed to become saturated for long periods. A good, free-draining house plant compost will help to prevent saturation and keep plants in good condition.

Opposite: A colourful specimen plant such as this fine codiaeum will brighten the corner of a hallway

CLIVIA MINIATA (Kafir Lily)

South Africa. September to April 10 to 13°C. (50 to 55°F.), April to September 16 to 18°C. (60 to 65°F.). Easy.

Only a few years ago the clivias were in very short supply and hardly worth mentioning because of their scarcity, but the supply situation has greatly improved and plants are now available from a number of specialist nurseries. The large, strap-like leaves of the clivia which are naturally glossy green make the plant attractive in itself, but added to this there is the excitement of a succession of orange-coloured flowers in the spring and early summer.

A slight drawback with these plants is the fact that they produce a substantial amount of root, so to get the best from them they need to be grown in relatively large pots. Because of the vigorous root system they also need a fairly rich and heavy compost. The nurseryman would use something akin to J.I.P.3 into which he would work a little dried cow manure. (A very old-fashioned commodity, but it works wonders for some of those plants which do better in a rich compost). Potting on should be done in February and, should additional plants be wanted, root clumps can be divided at this time and planted up individually in smaller pots. Keep just moist in winter and water freely at other times, and place the plants in a light position.

COBAEA SCANDENS (Cups and Saucers)

Mexico. Minimum 10°C. (50°F.). Easy.

For the owner of the new garden room wishing to fill the growing space quickly and cheaply in the first year this could well be one of the chosen plants. Easily grown from seed sown early in the spring they can become quite rampant in agreeable conditions. However, should growth be excessive for the garden room, plants can be put out in the garden where they are perfectly hardy during the summer months. Though perennial, these plants are best treated as annuals and disposed of at the end of the summer. Once established all that is required is to keep them well watered and fed in order to be successful. Pot plants into larger containers as soon as they have sufficient roots; this will ensure ample growth. Once in pots of 10-in. size regular feeding will maintain them in good condition.

COCOS WEDDELLIANA

Minimum 13°C. (55°F.). Moderately easy.

Truly miniature and one of the most graceful of all foliage plants, *Cocos weddelliana* has in recent years been in short supply. A regrettable state of affairs but, like all these attractive slow-growing plants, once the demand exceeds supply it is very difficult for the producer to catch up. However, having traced a supplier and persuaded him to part with a plant, the owner should provide a moist situation in a light, warm place. Water sparingly in winter and more freely at other times; good drainage is important so one should ensure that water soaks through the compost quite quickly after watering. Avoid the temptation to pot on too frequently, as fully mature plants several years old need only be in 7-in. pots. And plants do look so much more elegant when growing in pots that are in proportion to their leaf development.

CODIAEUM (Croton, Joseph's Coat)

South East Asia. Minimum 16°C. (60°F.). Difficult.

The common name gives a clue to the type of plant; and it is indeed a plant of many colours that outshines every other species in foliage colouring. For years now we have been advised

Clianthus puniceus albus

Coffea arabica, the coffee plant

that codiaeum is the proper name, but the old one of croton is still favourite with both nurseryman and general public.

There are many, many varieties to choose from when making a selection, and all of them will tax the skill of anyone providing less than ideal conditions. In order to retain colouring and, equally important, to preserve the lower leaves of the plant, it is essential that the minimum temperature mentioned above should be maintained, a few degrees more if this is possible. Also the plants should be in the lightest position possible where they can enjoy ample sunlight, otherwise they will quickly show their displeasure by losing much of their exotic colouring. Ample moisture at the roots also plays an important part; and drying out, be it only for a short time, will almost inevitably result in loss of lower leaves, which will also occur if the temperature is inadequate.

Some years ago we took a magnificent specimen of *Codiaeum reidii* to a flower show in May. On the second day of the show the temperature dropped well below the recommended 16°C. The plant, which stood about 10 ft. in height and was fully 6 ft. in diameter, showed no immediate ill effects, but back at the nursery, some seven days later it stood like a blasted oak: there was not a leaf to be seen, not so much as one. It was an expensive flower show.

Once established in their pots a regular programme of feeding must be adhered to, as plants quickly deteriorate from lack of nourishment. Winter feeding may also be necessary if plants are producing new leaves. For preference plants should be potted on into larger containers in the spring of the year using J.I.P.3. Pot fairly firmly and please ensure that the pot is well drained by first putting a few crocks in the bottom.

Some of the crotons, such as *C.* Pennick and *C. pictum*, are a little easier to manage but, on the whole, they should all be considered delicate and in need of the cultural conditions described. However, don't let these suggested conditions put you off trying, as they can be most rewarding and certainly the most colourful plants that will enhance any collection.

If conditions are hot and dry there is a little pest known as red spider mite that will almost certainly appear and will revel in the conditions provided. So, as a first precaution against this wee mite one should endeavour to keep the garden room, or the area surrounding the plant indoors, as moist as possible. Where conditions permit this will entail frequent spraying of the foliage with water, paying attention to the under as well as the topsides of the leaves.

One of the best controls for red spider is white oil (available as Redomite spraying oil) which should be mixed as directed and heavily sprayed onto the leaves, particular attention again being paid to the undersides. Besides controlling the red spider mite these white oil sprays will also greatly improve the general appearance of the plant. This applies to almost all the glossy-leaved foliage plants that one is likely to encounter, but it is wise to test on one or two plants or a single leaf as a precaution before using white oil too freely.

COFFEA ARABICA

Arabia. Minimum 16°C. (60°F.).
Moderately easy.

There is always an interest in growing such things as pineapples, cotton plants and oranges, and the coffee plant is no exception. The would-be grower should, however, take heed of the fact that ample space is required if these plants are to be grown to the stage at which they are likely to produce coffee beans. And the real attraction is in the berries, which are in the most attractive shades of mottled yellows and oranges. Inside the berries are two beans which are the coffee beans of commerce. New plants may be raised by sowing seed in a high temperature in the early part of the year. Alternatively, and probably more practically, they may be increased by means of cuttings propagated in warm conditions in early summer.

COLEUS

Tropical Africa, South East Asia.
Minimum 13°C. (55°F.). Easy.

In the main it is generally reckoned that the more colourful the foliage the more difficult the plant is likely to prove in cultivation, but there are exceptions to almost every rule and the coleus is just that. These plants may be raised from seed or by means of cuttings, but cuttings of named varieties are far and away the best bet as they produce plants in colour and habit which are much superior. Cuttings of firm young shoots root with little bother at almost any time of the year, and an interesting and varied collection of these plants can quite quickly be built up. When they become too large and overgrown they should be replaced; in fact, it is wise always to

A collection of mixed coleus

have a few young plants coming along for this purpose.

Growing a few on to make standard plants can give a collection a new dimension, and it is much easier than may at first appear. With some varieties it is quite possible to produce 4-ft. tall standards in the autumn from spring-struck cuttings. Do this by allowing one strong shoot to develop unchecked in the centre of the pot, and as side growths are produced pinch them back to about two joints. The main stem will become much stronger than it would if these shoots were completely removed. When about 3 ft. 6 in. tall the growing tip of the plant is removed and as new shoots are made they too should have their tips removed to encourage a more bushy habit. Some varieties are better suited to making standards than others, but they are inexpensive and a few experiments will add to the fun of growing plants.

Coleus need a light position and a temperature in the region of 16°C. (60°F.), moist conditions during the growing months and a little dryer at other times. Keeping them well fed is also helpful, but avoid overdoing it. Potting them into slightly larger pots will be necessary two or three times during the course of the season. J.I.P.3 compost will do them quite well. Standard plants should be well staked to prevent stems snapping as the plant becomes top heavy.

COLUMNEA

Tropical America. September to April 16 to 18°C. (60 to 65°F.), April to September 18 to 24°C. (65 to 75°F.). Difficult.

This is almost the perfect plant for hanging baskets. Closely matted leaves trail for several feet and colourful flowers of scarlet, or scarlet and yellow, are normally produced in great profusion in early summer. Adequate temperature is most essential and it is equally important that the compost should not be allowed to dry out at any time during the summer months; this will entail watering the basket daily, often two or three times a day if it is really hot.

Plants are started from cuttings a few inches in length taken early in the year and given good consistent heat to get the rooting process under way. When rooted insert two to four cuttings in 3½-in. pots, and when established put three or four pots in each hanging basket using a standard house plant mixture. In order to encourage production of flowers, which are sometimes reluctant, it is an advantage to keep the compost on the dry side just prior to the natural flowering time of the plant. Not bone dry by any means, just a little dryer than usual, and you will find

that the results can be much more spectacular.

The most common variety is *Columnea banksii*, but there are a number of other equally interesting sorts to be found if one is fortunate enough to come across them.

CRYPTANTHUS (Earth Stars)

Tropical America. Minimum 16°C. (60°F.). Easy.

For the plant grower with limited space these compact and slow-growing members of the bromeliad family can prove most rewarding.

Cryptanthus bivittatus, *C. beuckeri* and *C. acaulis* take up practically no room whatsoever. Adaptability is another point in their favour; they may be grown conventionally in pots, used in bottle gardens, planted in tropical rockery effects in the garden room, or used to make living mobiles – an interesting and amusing way of displaying them. To make a mobile an attractive section of tree branch or piece of ornamental bark should be selected. The plants should be removed from their pots and a good thickness of sphagnum moss tied to the roots before they are attached to the tree with a length of plastic-covered wire. They can also be added to made-up jungle trees which have all sorts of bromeliads, platyceriums and such like attached to them.

Any potting on is done into a very open, peaty mixture, and new plants are propagated from

Cryptanthus bromelioides tricolor

small offsets that appear at the base of the older plant. Building up stock is a slow business as plants produce very few of these offsets during the course of a growing season.

Compost should be free draining and never allowed to become too wet, while plants grown on jungle trees or mobiles will have to be damped over regularly to prevent them drying out excessively. If there is a container large enough the ideal arrangement for mobiles is to plunge them completely in water at regular intervals.

CUSSONIA SPICATA

Africa. 13 to 18°C. (55 to 65°F.). Easy.

These are tropical trees which can be raised from seed with little difficulty. During the first year they can be potted on several times and will benefit from this treatment, as growth and root development is very rapid.

The tall, slender stems become very brittle and plants must be handled extremely carefully when being moved – leaning them at a slight angle will be quite enough to break the stem. Fortunately new growth quickly reappears.

The foliage is plain green and leaf stalks and main stems of younger plants have an attractive bloom on them. Keep well watered, well fed and in good light, and they will quite quickly develop into small trees indoors.

CYCLAMEN

Syria. 10 to 13°C. (50 to 55°F.). Easy.

We are continually being told that centrally heated rooms are totally unsuited to this particular plant, and as accommodation of this kind is ever on the increase, you would think the demand for cyclamen must decline. Not so – plants are being produced in ever greater numbers. The simple reason is that people like cyclamen. It is as easy to understand as that. Often enough the customer comes into the plant centre and begins by mentioning that he, or more often she, cannot keep cyclamen, only to look around at the wealth of other plants on show and come back to the salesgirl rather sheepishly with another cyclamen apologetically saying, 'They are rather lovely.' Lovely or not, it really is a little foolish to purchase cyclamen and expect them to last if one lives in a very hot and dry centrally heated apartment. The conditions are so alien to what they have been accustomed to that they have only a marginal chance of survival for more than a limited length of time.

On the nursery, plants are grown in lightly shaded greenhouses which are rarely heated to more than 13°C. (55°F.). Except, of course, when the sun is shining and it is very hot outside; in these conditions the ventilators are opened to their fullest extent in order to keep the inside temperature as low as possible. If these light and airy conditions can be emulated indoors then there is every chance that one can succeed with these cool and beautiful plants. When watering, adopt the rule of giving a good watering and allowing the compost to dry a little before giving any more. Feed occasionally with a weak liquid fertiliser.

Cyclamen flower in winter, which could account for the continued popularity despite the difficulty of providing the right conditions in the modern home. They are available in many flower shades of pink, scarlet, mauve and white. Although they are usually a little more costly, the silver leaf strain of cyclamen is far superior to any of its predecessors and is well worth the little extra cost that will be involved.

Keeping cyclamen plants from one year to the next defeats many, perplexes many and satisfies a few. At the various flower shows we attend we meet many plant growers who have the most astonishing collection of problems. One lady informed me that she had tried for many years to keep her plants without success and after her experiences that year she had finally decided to give up. It seems that of two cyclamen corms that were kept one grew and produced nothing but leaves and the other corm produced a few flowers, but no leaves at all. It was probably as well that she accepted this as some sort of omen.

For those wishing to succeed, however, I cannot do better than quote the method adopted by the rather ancient gardener whose photograph appeared in a gardening magazine proudly holding his cyclamen corm for which he vouched the age was no less than sixty years. His method was, very simply, to grow the plant in a cool room and gradually to withhold water as the plant began to die back naturally until the compost in the pot was quite dry. About the middle of May he would place the plant in the greenhouse under the staging on its side to prevent water getting into the pot. It was left there until new growth was apparent about the end of June. The corm (almost turnip size) was then removed from the pot and all the compost shaken off before being replanted in the same pot in fresh compost. The plant was then gradually re-accustomed to indoor warmer conditions before frosts were likely.

Even so, no matter how well one may keep plants from year to year they are rarely as good as the new plants that the nurseryman raises from fresh seed sown annually in September, October and November.

CYPERUS (Umbrella Plant)

Africa. Minimum 13°C. (55°F.). Easy.

There are two kinds suitable as house or garden room plants: *Cyperus diffusus*, the smaller of the two, is more suited to the living room, while the tall and stately *C. alternifolius* will do better in more spacious surroundings. Both must have a lightly shaded position in which to grow and must be kept very moist at all times. In fact, these are two of the few indoor plants that will benefit if their plant pots are left standing in water. It can be a shallow dish or an ornamental pool.

C. diffusus is the tougher of the two and is hardy out of doors, but it is better to keep the plant reasonably warm in order to get freer and more attractive growth.

C. alternifolius, when growing in a pot, will attain a height of some 6 ft., and is much more at home when growing in, or around, a pool. Both plants get their common name of umbrella plant because of the umbrella-like flower that sprouts from the top of the flower stalks. These umbels, or umbrella tops, may be cut off with 3 or 4 in. of stem attached and used as cuttings for raising new plants; they may be rooted in water or in a propagating medium. New plants may also be raised from spring-sown seed, or more easily by dividing the clumps when they are large enough. Almost any time will do for this operation.

DATURA SUAVEOLENS (Trumpet Flower)

Mexico. September to April 4 to 10°C. (40 to 50°F.), April to September 13 to 18°C. (55 to 65°F.). Easy.

A word of warning here: this datura develops into a substantial shrub, attaining a height of 6 ft. plus when grown in large pots or tubs, so it is only suitable if adequate winter quarters can be provided. However, fragrant white flowers in the shape of pendulous trumpets make these plants a tempting proposition, and they are comparatively easy to grow.

Raised from cuttings about 6 in. in length, which can be taken at almost any time except in winter, and potted on into rich compost, they quickly make up into impressive plants. In winter the temperature can fall to 4°C. (40°F.) if water is given sparingly and the compost kept on the dry side, but a winter temperature nearer the 10°C. (50°F.) mark would be more suitable. From June to the end of September they may be placed out of doors on a terrace or patio; in decorative containers they are seen at their best and have ample room for development. A rich, fairly heavy compost is required when potting on. Whitefly can be troublesome and out of doors can be discouraged if not completely eradicated by frequent spraying of the undersides of leaves with a garden hose. Not many insecticides are effective against whitefly, but the water treatment will be a deterrent and is much less expensive! Following their summer season out of doors plants should be hard pruned before being reintroduced to the garden room or greenhouse. In this way many of the pests will find their way to the rubbish heap, and plants will occupy much less winter storage space.

DAVALLIA CANARIENSIS (Hare's-foot Fern)

Canary Is. Minimum 4°C. (40°F.). Easy.

Almost as much a part of the Victorian era as the aspidistra, the hare's-foot fern is not encountered very often today. Something of a pity, as this is one of the easiest possible plants to grow besides being rather interesting and to some extent amusing. For ferns the leaves are rather coarse and not very attractive, but the rhizomatous growth from which fronds emerge will always attract attention. These hairy rhizomes creep over the edge of the pot and look for all the world like hare's feet. Kept on the dry side in cool conditions in winter and watered and fed during the summer months, they present few problems. Having acquired one plant it is not difficult to increase by division of the rhizomes in the early part of the year. Grow them in pots or hanging baskets; when planted in hanging baskets they can take on a rather weird appearance in time.

DICKSONIA

Australia, New Zealand. Minimum 10°C. (50°F.). Moderately easy.

You will in all probability never be able to purchase one of these truly majestic and beautiful ferns, which may grow to a height of 15 to 20 ft. in their native habitat, but would rarely do so well in a greenhouse environment. They are mentioned here so that you may not miss the opportunity of seeking them out on the next botanic garden visit. Who knows, you may have an acquaintance with a botanic garden who has one to spare – it seems the only way of acquiring them.

Plants are usually grown in well-shaded, spacious greenhouses where the atmosphere is kept moist and the plants are sprayed over frequently.

DIEFFENBACHIA (Dumb Cane)

Tropical America. Minimum 13°C. (55°F.). Moderately easy and difficult.

Exotic is the word; the dieffenbachias are very much in the top league as far as decorative foliage plants are concerned. Some are a little easier to manage than others, but most will tax the skill of the most green-fingered of growers.

The following notes on general care apply to all the many different varieties likely to be encountered. Adequate heat is essential and the minimum temperature mentioned above would really be rock bottom; 16°C. (60°F.) would be more satisfactory. In the garden room light shading of the glass would be necessary, as well as the maintenance of a damp atmosphere. Water more freely in summer, and feed regularly with a liquid fertiliser. Potting on is best done between April and the end of June, using a standard house plant compost. New plants are propagated by means of stem cuttings, no leaves being required. The stems are cut up into sections about 3 in. long and allowed to dry before being placed on their sides on standard propagating compost and pressed firmly in. Kept in a close atmosphere at a temperature in the region of 22°C. (72°F.) they will root with reasonable ease. A strong word of warning here, however: it is extremely important that the sap from the plant does not accidentally get into one's mouth, so hands should be washed immediately after completing the propagating operation. The consequence of getting sap in the mouth is that the tongue swells up rendering one speechless – a particularly unpleasant experience. It is for this reason that the dieffenbachias have acquired their unusual common name of dumb cane. Keeping plants away from the inquisitive hands of children is therefore an important precaution.

Of the many different sorts that are available *Dieffenbachia arvida exotica* is the most popular for a number of reasons, not least because they are comparatively easy to grow both indoors and in the greenhouse, and when they reach maturity they are still neat, compact plants which are simple to pack for dispatch and not much trouble to handle. There is an improved variety at present named *D.* Perfection, the principal difference being that it produces a number of basal shoots around the main stem of the parent plant. Even in average conditions indoors this dieffenbachia has proved itself, and seems quite capable of withstanding considerable fluctuation in temperature – an advantage where central heating is only switched on at times when it is required. In 5-in. pots these plants attain a height of some 18 in., but by putting two or three in 7-in. pots plants of as much as 3 ft. can be grown.

D. amoena is much more robust, producing leaves 2 to 3 ft. in length and fully 15 in. wide, and can be a worthwhile addition to any plant collection. Plants may attain a height of 5 ft. or more, but this would only be expected in the most agreeable of conditions. Having reached their maximum height dieffenbachias begin to produce insignificant arum-like flowers (they belong to the arum family) but when this happens the plants will have lost much of their attraction and it is usually wise to cut them back and allow new growth to sprout from the base of the stem. These new shoots will have begun to grow by the time flowers develop. As flowers do nothing for the appearance of the plant they should be removed as they appear.

Introduced a few years ago, *D.* Tropic Snow is similar to *amoena* in habit of growth, but has much more variegated and stiffer leaves, which makes the plants more delicate to handle. However, in spite of the supposed improvement, my preference still lies with *amoena* which seems much less stiff and formal.

One of my favourites among the dieffenbachias is *D. oerstedii*, which has very dark green leaves with a centre mid-rib which is a complete contrast in a beautiful creamy white. Not everyone's choice and not likely to make the grade as a popular house plant, but an interesting subject, nevertheless, for anyone seeking the unusual. Equally unlikely to make the grade in the pot plant top ten is *D.* Pia, quite different from *oerstedii* in that the variegated leaves have practically no green in them at all. For exhibition work and startling effect when grouped together there are few plants that can be more effective. Because of the lack of chlorophyll in the leaves it has always been a difficult plant to manage, so we were more than pleased when we found what seemed to be at least a partial answer to the problem, an answer that could well apply to plants other than this dieffenbachia.

For an exhibition it was decided to group about nine plants of *D.* Pia in a container about 3 ft. in diameter. To keep them in position the pots were plunged in moist sphagnum peat. Following the exhibition the plants were returned to the nursery and, being an attractive arrangement, they were left in the large container. Some two years later the plants were still grouped together. They had grown to some 3 ft. 6 in. in height and, incredibly enough, had lost practically no leaves in this time, while similarly aged individual plants had long since passed their best. Later experiments with equally difficult plants were tried and it seemed proved beyond doubt that the majority fared very much better when placed in larger containers with moist sphagnum moss packed around the pots.

DIONAEA MUSCIPULA (Venus Fly Trap)

America. 4 to 13°C. (40 to 55°F.). Difficult.

These are insectivorous plants with sensitive leaf hairs which, when a fly lands on them, induce the leaf to close up slowly and trap the fly inside. The plant feeds on all manner of insects in this way and an incredible number of gullible people buy this plant fondly thinking that they are going to take it home and sit indoors watching this wonder of nature methodically gobbling up all the flies in the room. A few purchasers may well enjoy this treat, but for the few that do there must be many thousands who only see the leaves fold together when they poke them with a matchstick and in a short space of time watch the rapid decline of the plant.

Many plants are sold purely on account of a gimmick and this must surely be one of the most successful as far as the supplier is concerned – and one of the least successful from the point of view of the purchaser. Perhaps the information attached to the plant label may tell you how wonderfully well they will do on the ordinary window-sill, and what splendid fly catchers these amusing plants will prove to be. But, take it from me, that's just a lot of eyewash: these plants require conditions much more specialised than the average window ledge if they are to grow at all. Even when growing well in a specialised environment they are not particularly interesting. The best plants I have seen were growing in a large glass case and the plant pots were plunged to their rims in wet sphagnum moss. The only snag was that the perpetual moisture resulted in the glass misting over heavily making it impossible to see what was inside until the cover was removed. Still, one supposes that the owner may get as much pleasure from the occasional glance at his Venus fly traps as the stamp collector gets from the periodic visit to the safe deposit to inspect his treasures.

However, having been told how unsatisfactory they are as house plants many would-be purchasers will still not be deterred from at least giving them a try, so for those who won't take advice – let me offer a little more!

For compost use a mixture of equal parts peat and fresh sphagnum moss; fresh moss only, dry and dead moss will be of no use. When the plant has been potted, the pot should be plunged to its rim in a larger pot and the space between them should be packed around with wet moss. From then on it is important to keep the plant warm, shaded and moist; this can be done by spraying the foliage over regularly with a fine scent spray filled with tepid water. If at all possible the plant should be enclosed in a glass case of some kind. Finally, don't be forever poking at the leaves to make them close, as it does the plant no good whatsoever. The best advice really is try to refrain from buying them.

DIOSCOREA DISCOLOR (Variegated Yam)

Tropical America. Minimum 13°C. (55°F.). Difficult.

The yams are started from potato-like tubers and make excellent climbers for the garden room; in fact, in good conditions you can almost see them grow. When purchasing the dormant tubers it is most important to stipulate that you want only the variegated form, as the plain-leaved plants are not especially attractive. Having acquired the tubers it is again important to ensure that adequate heat is available for starting them into growth; a temperature around the pots in the region of 22°C. (72°F.) is about right. Start them in small pots or boxes filled with moist peat and transfer them to J.I.P.3 compost as soon as they have made a few leaves. Keep in reasonable heat until they have become established, then gradually accustom them to cooler conditions. As these plants grow rapidly moving them into larger pots should not be too long delayed. When in larger pots three or four canes at least 6 ft. in length should be inserted up which the vigorous growth can climb. Keep well watered, well fed and lightly shaded during the spring and summer. In late summer growth dies down quite naturally and the compost should then be kept dry, and the potful of tubers stored in a warm place until the following February, when the growing process can be started all over again. The dry tubers should be knocked out of the pot and the old soil discarded, fresh compost being used for the new potting operation.

DIPLADENIA

Tropical America. September to April 13 to 16°C. (55 to 60°F.), April to September 18 to 24°C. (65 to 75°F.). Difficult.

There are numerous different varieties of dipladenia, but the one the house plant grower will most likely come across is *Dipladenia rosea*, which grows less vigorously than most. These are best kept in a light position and, being natural climbers, some form of support should be provided for growth to twine around. Use a peaty compost when potting and a weak liquid fertiliser once plants have become established in their pots. Indoors, where growth is less active, it will be better if the growing temperature can be maintained in the region of 18°C. (65°F.); the higher temperature will be more suitable for the

119

garden room where growth is usually stronger.

Of the more vigorous plants available the white form, *D. boliviensis*, will tolerate lower temperatures and will, therefore, be more suited to less agreeable conditions. Plants can be trimmed back at the end of the season, and during the winter they ought to be kept on the dry side. In common with almost all greenhouse plants which have tightly matted, twining stems mealy bug can be troublesome when it gets in among the branches and is difficult to contact effectively when spraying. A regular inspection of plants should be made and necessary precautions taken at the first sign of trouble.

DIZYGOTHECA ELEGANTISSIMA
(Spider Plant)

Pacific Isles. 18°C. (65°F.). Difficult.

The lads who name our plants do indeed present us with what appear to be unnecessary problems at times, and this would seem to be one of the times. All over the world this plant is known to almost everyone with an interest in indoor plants as *Aralia elegantissima*, but the heading name is more correct, so you will have to put up with it. Anyway, as the great man said, 'What's in a name?' *Elegantissima* is, whatever else may be said, eminently suitable, as this must be one of the most attractive of plants, having dark green, almost black, filigreed foliage which never looks better than when set off in white-painted surroundings. As a solitary specimen or as part of a group, it is an invaluable display plant.

Not by any means an easy plant to care for, it must have warmth, light shade and, in particular, careful watering. If compost remains wet for long periods, especially in winter, it will almost inevitably result in leaves showering off. However, it must be said that in agreeable conditions they grow very well and scale insects appear to be the only pests that show any real interest in them.

In ideal conditions they can develop into substantial trees some 20 ft. in height, but leaves coarsen and they lose much of their elegant appearance in the growing process. Even in the greenhouse, as plants increase in height, there is a marked tendency for them to shed lower leaves and one is left with a tall umbrella effect. However, being an accommodating sort of plant, the main stems can be cut back to more manageable height and new growth will appear around the point of severence. At first the bare stumps will seem an odd sight, but have no fear, they will in time grow new leaves. Do the cutting back in the early part of the year. New plants can be raised from seed in the spring.

DRACAENA

**Tropics. Minimum 10 to 18°C. (50 to 65°F.).
Easy and difficult.**

These are divided into two groups, dracaenas and cordylines, but the majority are sold as the former, so we will risk offending and class them all as dracaenas. Very different in their appearance and in their requirements, it is not possible to lump them all together and give general advice concerning culture, so they will have to be taken individually.

Dracaena deremensis and *D. d. bausei* are similar in appearance and requirements, both needing light shading and a temperature in the region of 18°C. (65°F.). Both have a maximum height when grown in pots of 8 to 10 ft., by which time they will have lost most of their lower leaves and will be growing with slender stems and tufted growth at the top. Losing the lower leaves in this way is a characteristic of dracaenas of this type, and does not detract too much from their appearance as the stems in themselves are not unattractive. In order to encourage plants of more interesting shape the growing tops can be removed when they are about 3 ft. in height; with luck several stems should result. Of the two *D. bausei* is the more colourful, having a distinctive white-centred leaf, but alas, it is also a little more difficult to care for. These taller growing plants must have a substantial root system if they are to remain anchored to the ground, so they will need potting on into slightly larger containers in the spring of each year, using a fairly heavy compost which will keep them going for the twelve months.

D. godseffiana Florida Beauty is an entirely different plant in appearance and is much more suitable for room decoration; leaves are smaller and much more numerous and the plant has an overall golden appearance. The improved type is considerably more attractive than *D. godseffiana*, which has dull green leaves faintly speckled with white. Not easy to grow (many of my professional colleagues consider them difficult), we have found that by planting from six to nine of these in earthenware saucers some 3 ft. in diameter and 6 in. in depth they grow extremely well. In the larger area plants have a much better root run and respond by growing to a height of 3 or 4 ft., which is unusually tall for this variety. Plants placed in offices in such containers also give much better results than those growing in more conventional pots. Temperature and general conditions should be similar to that recommended for the first two dracaenas.

D. marginata has red-margined spiky green leaves and attains a height of some 15 to 20 ft. when growing in a pot. However, it is a slow business which may take as much as ten years, and should they outgrow their headroom it is a simple business to halt their upward progress temporarily by removing the growing tip of the plant. One of the easiest of all the dracaenas to care for, a minimum temperature in the region of 10°C. (50°F.) is advised, though it tolerates higher temperatures quite happily. Keep lightly shaded and water only when necessary, particularly in winter when permanently saturated compost can put an end to the plant.

Removing the growing point (you can use it for propagating a new plant) at an early stage is

Dracaena marginata concinna

Right: *Dracaena massangeana*

a decided advantage with this plant, as you will get two or more stems which give the plant a nice weirdy look as it increases in height. This is one of the few plants I know that has the odd built-in arrangement for removing its own growing point in order to restrict the upward growth. This happens when the topmost leaves exude a sticky substance that holds them tightly together, and as the plant continues to grow and the leaves cannot unfold the top of the plant snaps off as cleanly as the proverbial whistle.

The silver-grey stems of several plants grouped together can be a rare sight for anyone appreciating the time and effort that goes into growing them. We have such a group on the nursery and I should say that almost every architect and florist who visits us enquires about purchasing it. But there are some things, even when you are commercially minded, that you have no wish to sell. We have a theory that the larger, more mature plants sell the smaller ones and it is certainly borne out in this instance, for we sell a number of smaller plants of *D. marginata*

for the architect or florist to plant up his own group – with our rather grand not-for-sale ones at the back of his mind!

This is one of my favourite plants, and I would suggest that should you have the space a few of these planted in an attractive container may not be such a bad idea, especially if the plants are varied in height.

Having seen so many promising new plants make their debut as potential contenders in the house plant stakes one tends to treat all new arrivals on the scene with a certain amount of scepticism. Therefore, one feels that there must be something special about the comparatively new variety, *Dracaena marginata concinna*, the rainbow plant, which has been greeted with considerable enthusiasm since it has become available. As the common name suggests the leaves are much more colourful than the green form, yet it seems to be no more difficult to care for. The stiff, russet-coloured leaves will surely have considerable appeal for the keen flower arranger, as well as the plantsman wishing to add something special to his collection. In common with *D. marginata* this plant can be allowed to grow as a tall single-stemmed individualist, or it may have the growing top removed in order to produce a more interesting plant with numerous shoots. If reasonably firm, the top section with at least 4 in. of stem may be inserted as a cutting if an extra plant is wanted.

D. massangeana, with wide, strap-like leaves that are a dull mustard and pale green in colour, requires similar conditions to the first-mentioned pair in the way of care and attention. An altogether much bolder plant than the others, it attains a maximum height of some 7 ft., but may produce a rather grand flowering stem at the top before it reaches its maximum height. The emergence of the flower spike is usually an indication that the plant should be cut down and used for propagating a few fresh plants, as it loses much of its appearance when producing flowers. Cuttings of stems that would seem too old for this purpose root with little difficulty.

D. sanderiana is an altogether smaller, much neater plant and therefore much more suitable for the average home. The treatment is more or less that suggested for the *deremensis* species.

Growth is upright and leaves are white and light grey in colour, making the plants very useful for incorporating in mixed arrangements where there is a backing of green plants, as is so often the case.

D. Rededge and *D. terminalis* have similar colouring of bright red and need much the same sort of treatment indoors: a light room with protection from direct sunlight and cool, moist conditions at their roots – plunging them in a container of moss as advised for *Dieffenbachia* Pia is a suggestion that may well be adopted. A final point with the dracaenas is that there seems

Dracaena sanderiana

to be a decided advantage in using rain or soft water when watering, a job that should be done thoroughly and the plant allowed to dry out a little before repeating.

ECHEVERIA

Mexico. September to April 4 to 10°C. (40 to 50°F.), April to September 13 to 16°C. (55 to 60°F.). Easy.

Not strictly house plants, the echeverias are succulents which are little trouble to care for and do very well on the light, sunny window ledge.

This is another species to which anyone who wishes to build up a collection of interesting and unusual plants may well turn his attention. All have fleshy leaves in shades of blue, grey and green, many of them seeming to change colour as the light strikes them from different directions. Added to this the majority will oblige during the summer months with flowers in shades of orange, red and yellow.

Propagation is by means of seed sown in March, or from cuttings taken in late summer. The cuttings are prepared from individual leaves; it is important to remove the complete leaf with the base attached, rather than cut through the leaf in order to remove it from the plant. Insert the cuttings in sandy, well-drained compost, and keep water off the leaves and the compost dry until growth is evident. When potting plants on into larger containers a cactus potting compost should be used, as it is important that there should be free drainage. Over the winter months plants will need very little water. More liberal watering should gradually be started early in March.

Many varieties are used for bedding out in the summer, and all of them may be placed out of doors when the weather is warmer.

Epiphyllum hybrid

EPIPHYLLUM

**Tropical America. September to April
4 to 10°C. (40 to 50°F.), April to September
10 to 16°C. (50 to 60°F.). Easy.**

Epiphyllums require very similar conditions to those described above for echeverias and, like them, they may be placed out of doors in a sheltered, sunny position during the warmer months of the year.

In appearance, however, the leaves are very different to the rosette-forming leaves of the echeveria. The epiphyllum has much longer leaves, either flat or slightly triangular in shape. They are not particularly attractive, but any deficiency in foliage appeal is more than compensated for in the flowers which are brilliantly colourful. In recent years epiphyllums have become much more popular and as a result there are many new hybrids available, and there is little doubt that they would provide considerable interest for anyone wishing to specialise. New plants can be raised from seed or from leaf sections a few inches in length inserted in sandy compost. Cuttings may be taken at almost any time if the conditions are favourable.

EPISCIA

**Tropical America. Minimum 13°C.
(55°F.). Moderately easy.**

Compact, warmth-loving plants which can be used for a variety of purposes if the temperature is adequate. A minimum of 13°C. (55°F.) is suggested, but plants will do better if 16°C. (60°F.) or a little above can be provided. They are quite useful in pots, but at their best when several are planted in a hanging basket, or when used as ground cover among other plants. Maintaining a moist atmosphere is an advantage, and will greatly encourage growth if plants are used

Episcia cupreata
Silver Queen

as ground cover. Leaves are primarily a mottled dark green in colour but develop interesting shades of pink in some growing conditions. They are very easy to propagate from cuttings, which usually entails nothing more than detaching from the parent plant pieces that have rooted into the peat, gravel or other plant pots surrounding the containers in which the episcias are growing. Keep on the dry side in winter, feed in summer and renew plants every second year or thereabouts, as young plants are so much more attractive and vigorous than the older ones. They can look much more effective if a seed box is filled with potting compost and twenty or so cuttings are rooted in the compost and allowed to grow there rather than being transplanted into pots in the conventional way.

EUCALYPTUS (Gum)

Australia. September to April 4 to 10°C. (40 to 50°F.), April to September 13 to 16°C. (55 to 60°F.). Easy.

Slightly tender evergreens which may be planted out of doors during the summer months, or more permanently in milder areas, eucalyptus are also useful as indoor plants where there is adequate light and the temperature is not too high. Raised from seed sown in March in a temperature in the region of 18°C. (65°F.), they require more or less standard treatment for plants preferring

Euphorbia tannanarive

a light, cool position. Pinch out the growing tip to encourage a more bushy shape, and don't be too disappointed if what seem to be perfectly healthy plants should suddenly collapse and die for no apparent reason; it appears to be a peculiarity of many of the eucalyptus. On the whole, however, they are not too troublesome.

EUCHARIS

Tropical America. Minimum 13°C. (55°F.). Easy.

Many of these lilies are easy to care for, strikingly beautiful and capable of enhancing the appearance of any plant collection. The flowers of the white eucharis lily are just about as white as white can be; a small collection of bulbs will provide a number of flowers from mid-summer into the autumn. These look better in smaller pots and three bulbs planted firmly in J.I.P.3 in April–May will give excellent results in 5-in. pots. Increase from offsets removed at potting-time or much more slowly from seed sown in good heat early in the year.

EUONYMUS (Spindle-tree)

Japan. Hardy. Easy.

The odd eyebrow may be raised at the sight of this plant in the pages of a house plant book, but peculiar things happen in the plant world and the house plant growers have discovered that *Euonymus japonicus aureus* makes a perfectly acceptable indoor plant which is comparatively easy to care for. And if it does shed its lower leaves and lose much of its attraction all is not lost: it can always be planted in the garden shrubbery to grow again another day. Very few problems here; grow in a light, cool position, avoiding excessive heat at all costs, water in moderation and it should not be too troublesome. It is easily propagated from cuttings a few inches in length at any time other than the winter months of the year.

EUPHORBIA

Mexico, Madagascar. September to April 7 to 10°C. (45 to 50°F.), April to September 13 to 16°C. (55 to 60°F.). Easy.

Several euphorbias are of interest to the house plant grower (not least the poinsettia, listed separately) and *Euphorbia splendens*, crown of thorns, is one of the most popular. It requires good light, compost that is never too wet, regular pinching of the leading growth, and pots that are not out of proportion to the size of the plant, and it will go on for years. Small, bright red flowers are produced for several months in summer, but not on plants that have permanently saturated compost – keep the compost on the dry side and they will flower much more freely. Propagation is from cuttings 4 or 5 in. in length; remove these carefully to prevent damage from the vicious spines that cover the plant, and allow the severed ends of the cuttings to dry for at least one day before inserting them in compost that is on the dry side in a temperature of not less than 16°C. (60°F.).

E. milii is more compact and a neater plant requiring similar conditions to *E. splendens*, but it is a much more difficult plant to care for, and is not really suitable for the beginner. *E. tannanarive* is another very similar plant with yellow flowers which can be particularly attractive on more mature plants. Here again, however, it is not easy. The latter two would do better if the minimum temperature did not fall below 13°C. (55°F.).

E. fulgens is a much more graceful plant which does not have the spiteful barbs of those previously mentioned. It also has the most exquisite orange-coloured flowers that are produced under normal conditions in February. By controlling the amount of light available they may be induced to flower in time for Christmas, which can be a considerable advantage to the commercial grower.

The common name of stick plant describes admirably the appearance of *Euphorbia tirucalli* which is composed of countless interwoven stick-like stems that provide an interesting and not unattractive plant. When planted out in the greenhouse border it quickly develops into a substantial plant, but can be kept to a reasonable size when the roots are confined to a pot and is one of the easiest plants to manage in any well-lit situation where the temperature is in the region of 10°C. (50°F.). If need be it will go for many weeks with no need for water, and in this respect seems to be almost as tough as the mother-in-law's tongue, so may well be the ideal plant for the beginner to contemplate growing.

Annual potting on into J.I.P.3 compost is recommended until the plant is in a 7-in. pot; thereafter it can be sustained for several years by regular feeding. Should the plant become too large for any particular situation it can be trimmed to shape quite severely at any time.

EXACUM AFFINE

Socotra. Minimum 13°C. (55°F.). Easy.

These are attractive little plants with crisp, clean foliage and masses of pale blue flowers which appear for several months from midsummer onwards. Culture is pretty well standard as for house plants which prefer a light, cool position in which to grow. Raised from seed

Exacum affine

sown in March–April and gradually potted on as required, *E. affine* is perennial and can be propagated from cuttings, but is best treated as an annual which will give fresh plants each year.

FATSHEDERA LIZEI

Garden origin. Minimum 10°C. (50°F.). Easy.

These plants will survive in much lower temperatures, and are indeed hardy out of doors in milder regions, but they will do better as pot plants if the suggested minimum is adhered to. Once attuned to higher temperatures in the seventies they settle down quite happily. They are interesting in that they are a combination of two plants, *Fatsia japonica* and *hedera*, hence the appropriate name of fatshedera. Essentially erect growing, they seem to go on growing for evermore in good conditions; I can think of several that wind their way up staircases, around picture frames and goodness knows where else.

Give them reasonable light and standard

One of the ferns,
Nephrolepis Whitnarii

treatment for the easier sort of plant and they are not too bothersome. One important precaution is to ensure that the leaves are not cleaned with any sort of oil preparation, as leaves of this plant are particularly susceptible to damage from such treatment. A soft sponge and water only should be used when cleaning leaves.

Propagation can be done vegetatively from single leaves with a piece of stem attached, or from the top 5 in. of the plant provided the leaves are not too soft; any time of the year will do if the temperature is adequate. One can also make interesting plants by grafting tops of young ivy plants about 3 in. long on to the fatshedera. Beautiful standard effects can be obtained by grafting three or four ivies on to the top of a fatshedera and, when the grafts have taken, removing all the leaves from the fatshedera.

FERNS

Moderately easy.

Some of the ferns have been listed individually, but it would be impossible to treat them all similarly, so some general advice is given on the care and attention relevant to the majority of them. They include so many beautiful and delicate foliage plants that it is a wonder they are not much more popular than they are. One very obvious reason is that in the plant trade ferns have a somewhat cheap image and rarely achieve their true value when sent to market. On the nursery they require much warmer and more specialised conditions, on the whole, than the majority of indoor plants though these, strangely enough, realise a better price when marketed.

The smaller ferns, selaginellas, for example, are ideal subjects and often grow very much better in small glass cases where an agreeable environment can be created. Warmer conditions are needed for starting them off, then for most of them moist, cool and shaded conditions are best for growing them on.

FICUS

Tropical regions. Easy and difficult.

All over the world there must be millions of ficus grown annually for indoor decoration, ranging from the tiny creeping fig, *Ficus pumila*, to majestic trees of *F. benjamina* and *F. benghalensis*. None of them flower when grown in pots, so the attraction is entirely in the foliage.

Ficus elastica robusta is the now greatly improved ordinary rubber plant which is produced in vast quantities annually. We often hear it said that they are falling off in popularity, but this is

128

totally untrue as there are more and more grown each year. Although it is still referred to as the ordinary rubber plant the *robusta* variety is a good example of the way in which many indoor plants are improved out of recognition almost unnoticed. Compared to its predecessors, *F. elastica* and *F. e. decora*, the *robusta* is a far superior and much stronger plant; one has only to see the three placed side by side to appreciate the tremendous improvement.

Even so, we still get masses of dead leaves sent through the post and placed in our hands at flower shows by rubber plant owners who just cannot understand where they have gone wrong. If the plant pot accompanies the leaves, as it often does, the reason for the plant's dilemma is in most cases found in the compost, which is much too wet. Very wet soil that rarely has a chance to dry out must inevitably result in the inactive roots dying off, and the consequence of this is the eventual loss of leaves. The sad thing is that when plants lose leaves as a result of wet compost and dead roots the owner stretches out an instinctive hand for the watering-can and, instead of keeping the sick plant on the dry side as it should be, saturates it even more. When plants are sick – and this advice is pretty well general for them all – they should be kept on the dry side, should not be fed until they show signs of recovery, and on no account should any attempt be made to pot them on into larger pots. Disturbance of the already damaged roots by repotting can be absolutely fatal.

For best results the rubber plant should enjoy a temperature of between 10°C. (50°F.) and 16°C. (60°F.). Higher temperatures result in weak, droopy growth and generally sick-looking plants. And it is not especially beneficial to pot the plant into a larger pot too frequently. It can be sustained for several years in the same pot once it has reached the 7- and 10-in. sizes. Tiny plants in huge pots seldom do well either in the expert's greenhouse or in the average home.

Advice is often sought about what should be done with plants that are almost touching the ceiling, and the expert's advice is sometimes rather shattering. Some years ago on a radio gardening programme a questioner asked what to do with her rubber plant that had outgrown its setting. Several ideas were offered, then one of the panel of experts suggested removing a yard or so out of the centre of the plant, and making a V-shaped cut in the stump and a wedge-shaped cut in the top section. The wedge would then be placed in the V-cut, tied in position, and a stake inserted to support the plant. Next day my curiosity got the better of me and an old rubber plant with no leaves on the lower section duly had its middle removed and the shortening procedure was executed. The plant did not so much as flag; the top and lower sections married perfectly and the only indication that something odd had taken place was a slight swelling at the point of union and a few curious aerial roots which had pushed out of the main stem of the top section. It was probably wondering what was going on, as well it might! Anyway, for what it is worth, that is one sure-fire way of reducing the height of a leggy rubber plant.

Ficus benjamina (weeping fig), *F. lyrata* and the smaller *F. pumila* and *F. radicans variegata* require higher temperatures than the ordinary rubber plant, not less than 16°C. (60°F.), with a maximum temperature in the region of 22°C. (72°F.).

F. benjamina will eventually develop into tree proportions, by which time it will have the trunk of a young sapling and most attractive white bark. Plants of this size take many years to grow and one should not purchase small plants with visions of them pushing out through the ceiling by the end of the year; growth indoors is considerably slower than in the greenhouse. When first introduced to a new environment the weeping fig has a disturbing habit of producing yellow leaves which it eventually sheds. However, unless the conditions of its new home are

very much against the plant it soon settles down.

Because of the leaf shape the fiddle-leaf fig is the common name given to *F. lyrata*, and very appropriate it is as the leaf clearly resembles a violin body. Leaves are of light green colouring and heavy veins of paler green single this plant out as one of the aristocrats of the purely green-foliaged house plants. Not an easy plant for the beginner but, nevertheless, most attractive when it is happy with its lot.

F. pumila and *F. radicans variegata* are a complete contrast to the previous two. Both have small leaves, the *pumila* a pleasant shade of green and the *radicans* variegated as the name suggests. These are fine for including in arrangements of assorted plants and equally good for ground cover between and in front of other pots in the garden room. Keep them moist, warm and out of direct sunlight, and pinch out the ends of leading growth occasionally to improve the general shape.

Another ficus for slightly warmer conditions is *F. diversifolia* which is slow growing and attractive mainly on account of the masses of small berries which are evident from the time the plants start into growth as small cuttings. Berries are somewhat anaemic in colouring, but interesting nonetheless.

Opposite:
Ficus benjamina, the weeping fig

Ficus radicans variegata

FITTONIA

**Tropical America. Minimum 16°C. (60°F.).
Difficult.**

There are only two fittonias likely to be offered
for sale, *Fittonia argyroneura* and *F. verschaffeltii,* both of which will tax the skill of the most
experienced plantsman. Both are frequently
given the common name of herring-bone plant,
on account of the intricate pattern of veins on the
upper surface of the leaf reminiscent of a herring
bone. In the case of *F. verschaffeltii* the pattern
is set against a reddish-brown background, and
in *F. argyroneura* the colouring is silver and pale
green. There is also a form *F. gigantea* which is
little more than a smaller leaved form of *F.
verschaffeltii,* but less attractive, so not a plant
to be sought after.

All three will require a moist, warm, shaded
environment in which to grow, and even then
will not be easy to manage. Indoors they would
be best suited to the atmosphere created in a
bottle garden, or enclosed glass case. (In
Victorian times these were referred to as Wardian
Cases, named after Nathaniel Ward who in-
vented them – in effect they were miniature
indoor greenhouses where one could grow plants
of a delicate nature). In the garden room it would
be essential to provide a warm bed of moist peat
in which to plunge the plant pots. Provided the
surroundings are shaded the maximum temperature is unimportant so long as it does not
rise above 27°C. (80°F.). Propagate from stem
cuttings with two to three leaves attached.

FUCHSIA

**Mainly Tropical America. 4 to 18°C. (40
to 65°F.). Easy.**

For my money there is no plant to touch the
fuchsia for garden room or greenhouse display;
they are very little trouble, reasonably priced,
easily propagated and go on flowering from early
spring right through until late summer. However, one must agree that they make poor
permanent house plants, having an annoying
habit of shedding their flowers soon after introduction to most indoor environments, as they
prefer light, airy conditions. Allowing for the
fact that they may prove problematical indoors
they are still superb plants for the greenhouse,
garden room, or for planting in the garden as
temporary or permanent residents, depending
on whether they are hardy or not.

There are obviously ideal times for propagating cuttings but my experience is that when
someone gives you a healthy cutting of a particularly good variety it will root at almost any

time if the conditions are right: warm, lightly
shaded and moist.

Supremely adaptable, fuchsias may be used as
conventional pot plants, as climbers or in hanging baskets. A glance through any good nursery
catalogue on fuchsias will indicate the treatment
that suits a particular variety best. Plant them
in J.I.P.3 compost, feed them well when established, air the house freely on hot days and you
cannot help but succeed. In hanging baskets they
are probably seen to best advantage, and one
need not go through the usual performance of
gradually potting cuttings into larger pots and
then planting them in the baskets when considered large enough. Instead try rooting the
cuttings in 3-in. pots, allow them to become
established, then pot directly around the edge of
the basket with 5 or 6 in. between each potful.
The size of the basket is immaterial provided the
compost does not become too wet before the
cuttings get under way. This advice may seem
to go against the book, but it works and the
cuttings will be in their permanent home much
sooner than usual and the display will be just as
good and weeks ahead of normal.

Fuchsias quickly develop into large plants and,
unless one has ample space for overwintering
them, it is usually better to take cuttings towards
the end of the summer to be grown on the
following year, keeping only a few of the older
plants. There are so many excellent varieties it
seems pointless to list them here when any good
catalogue will give pictures, names and the
particular treatment that certain kinds should
have in order to obtain best results.

Standard plants can be grown in twelve to
eighteen months by following the advice given
for producing coleus standards. Once established, plants of this kind and all older plants can
be kept for many years by removing most of the
old compost early in the year and repotting in
fresh J.I.P.3.

FURCRAEA

**Tropical America. September to April
10 to 13°C. (50 to 55°F.), April to September
13 to 18°C. (55 to 65°F.). Easy.**

The furcraeas are fairly easy to manage if the
compost is kept on the dry side all the time; too
wet and the edges of leaves will develop unsightly brown patches that in time result in the
loss of the entire leaf. And being rosette-forming
plants the loss of any established leaf will mar
the overall appearance of the plant. Warm, dry
and light conditions are best. Plants have
attractive variegated, fleshy leaves with spiteful
spines along their edge at intervals, so potting

on must be done with some care. In any event, pots will require to be housed where there is ample space because of the widely spreading leaves.

The plant which is most frequently seen is *Furcraea selloa marginata*, but there is also a form with smoother edges to the leaves, *F. foetida*. More difficult to obtain, it is well worth acquiring should the opportunity arise.

GARDENIA JASMINOIDES (Cape Jasmine)

China, Japan. September to March 13 to 18°C. (55 to 65°F.), March to September 18 to 24°C. (65 to 75°F.). Moderately easy.

There are a number of others available, but this is the species most frequently met with. Healthy plants develop into compact bushes of glossy green leaves, producing double white flowers with an almost overpowering scent during the summer months, and for this reason alone they are worthy of inclusion in a collection of plants. It will be noted that the foregoing sentence is qualified with the important words 'healthy plants'; so many plants are the complete opposite and have little chance of producing anything but the odd few distorted flowers.

Chlorotic (yellowing) condition of the leaves, due to an alkaline compost, causes much of the trouble, so it is important to use a suitable mixture at the beginning and when potting plants on into larger pots. The condition can usually be rectified by applying sequestered iron according to the manufacturer's directions. Most good garden shops will be able to supply sequestered iron.

Efforts should be made to lay on a supply of rain water. Less water is needed when the plant is resting, but it is necessary to keep it moist at other times. Besides being moist at the roots, regular spraying over of the foliage is also beneficial, but care should be taken not to damage any flowers that may be open.

Premature loss of buds and flowers is a familiar complaint, and much of it is due to wide variations in general conditions, be it excessive fluctuation in temperature or the amount of

Gardenia jasminoides

water given to the plant. It is essential that compost should be free draining.

GLORIOSA

Tropical Africa. September to February 13 to 16°C. (55 to 60°F.), February to September 16 to 22°C. (60 to 71°F.). Easy.

Exotically flowered, tuberous-rooted climbing plants which are not difficult if temperature and conditions are satisfactory. In February put five to eight tubers to each 10-in. pot in J.I.P.3 compost, planting them about 3 in. deep. Water in, then keep the compost on the dry side until growth is evident when more liberal watering can gradually be started. After flowering the process should be reversed and the compost kept quite dry until tubers are repotted into fresh compost the following February. Provide some sort of framework for the growth to cling to, either in the actual pot or attached to a wall with the pot placed immediately below. Propagate from seed sown in good heat in February, or from offsets of older tubers when they are potted.

GLOXINIA (SINNINGIA)

Tropical America. 13 to 18°C. (55 to 65°F.). Easy.

For the experimentally minded grower this could well be an interesting plant, as any piece of leaf or stem seems quite prepared to produce plants. However, the best means of raising new plants is undoubtedly by sowing seed very thinly on the surface of a peat and sand mixture in the spring of the year; from such sowings excellent plants will be available in August or thereabouts. When they have attained reasonable size the seedlings can be planted directly into 5-in. half-pots filled with a mixture similar to that suggested for saintpaulias. For most of the squat plants that are similar to gloxinias the half-pots are proportionately right, and plants seem more attractive. After flowering the foliage will die down quite naturally, and water should be withheld and the tubers kept dry until they are repotted in the spring.

GREVILLEA ROBUSTA (Silk Oak)

Australia. 10 to 18°C. (50 to 65°F.). Easy.

It is surprising that this easily grown plant has not become much more popular with the house plant buying public over the years. Quick growing, upright growth and silky green leaves would seem to be a good success combination, but you

Gloriosa rothschildiana

Bottom: Gloxinia (sinningia) hybrid

Opposite: The flowers
of gloxinia (left
foreground),
marguerite
(*Chrysanthemum
frutescens*),
schizanthus, and the
tall *Clerodendrum
thomsoniae* blend well
with the richly
variegated leaves of
three varieties of coleus

just cannot tell with Mr Public. Light and airy surroundings plus standard house plant treatment will ensure success. Being fairly rapid in growth they should be potted on annually using J.I.P.3, and a little extra feeding will help. Easily propagated from seed sown in heat in March, or from cuttings taken with a heel of the old wood in the spring.

GYNURA

South East Asia. 10 to 16°C. (50 to 60°F.). Easy.

There are two sorts likely to be offered for sale, *Gynura aurantiaca* and *G. sarmentosa*. The latter has smaller leaves and is an altogether neater and more attractive plant, so the one to choose if there is a preference. When the light catches the leaves at the right angle they are the most incredible purple colour and the plants sell on sight. There are two snags, however; as they age the plants quickly become ragged and lose their attraction, and the orange-yellow flowers when they appear have such an offensive stench that it is quite enough to put anyone off. During the summer months the plants flower freely and it is a major problem for anyone in charge of a greenhouse to keep the flowers in check in order to make life a little more bearable. Have the plants by all means, but do pinch out the flowers. No special treatment is required. It is advisable to raise new plants regularly and dispose of older ones as they deteriorate. Cuttings are easily rooted.

Grevillea robusta

HEDERA (Ivy)

7 to 16°C. (45 to 60°F.). Easy.

Whatever else may be said of the ivies there is no lack of choice, and they can be adapted to many uses other than growing in very hot conditions. As far as possible a maximum temperature in the region of 16°C. (60°F.) should be the aim, as higher temperatures will almost inevitably result in leaves drying out and in time falling off. A cool, lightly shaded position in the room or garden room is ideal, with compost which is, if anything, inclined to be on the dry side. Stuffy conditions are also detrimental so, in warmer rooms, the windows ought to be opened occasionally to allow the circulation of fresh air.

Ivies may be used for almost every purpose, as trailing plants, upright plants on stakes, climbing plants against the wall or, very effectively, as hanging basket plants. In this respect they may be used in conjunction with other plants, or as individual specimens filling the basket. Grown in this way they should be treated as all individual plants used for basket work: a number of young plants are put in the basket at the outset to ensure a full appearance when plants mature.

Almost all ivies offered for sale as house plants can be acclimatised to outdoor conditions. Plant them out early in the summer to give them a chance to settle before the winter sets in. They may be planted out as ground cover amongst other plants, or planted near a wall to which they will naturally cling; there should be little need to warn that when so used plants will have to be severely pruned periodically to prevent them becoming too invasive. One of the very best as a climbing plant is *Hedera* Jubilee (Golden Heart), which makes a rather thin and scraggy pot plant, but when the golden foliage is seen against a wall in the sunlight the effect can be most appealing.

In spite of the vast number of plants which are much more attractive in appearance a surprising number of green-leaved ivies still retain their popularity. The fact that there are so many other colourful plants on the market is in all probability a very good reason for the continued appeal of the green varieties, as they are useful for toning down the colouring when planted arrangements are being prepared. *H.* Chicago has simple-shaped green leaves with no frills whatsoever. *H.* Green Ripple has slightly larger green leaves with prominent veins which are the main attraction. As the name suggests, *H.* Mini Green has smaller, more congested leaves that are crinkled at the edges.

Of the variegated plants for outdoor use, and

Hedera helix Adam

as durable indoor plants, the best small-leaved ivies are those with basically grey colouring. Of these *H.* Glacier is easily the toughest and is an excellent subject for finishing off the front of borders indoors and out, and in particular for use along the edge of outdoor window boxes. The rate of growth can be quite phenomenal; less than ten years ago we used *H.* Glacier to edge a bed of geraniums outside a store shed and, in spite of constant removal of cuttings for propagation, the building has almost disappeared beneath a raised carpet of ivy foliage. *H.* Heisse is very similar at first glance, but will be found to be a more attractive plant which does not have the coarseness of the Glacier variety. The best of the grey-foliaged ones are *H.* Adam and *H.* Little Diamond, both of which are very popular and, because of the demand, seem to be forever in short supply. The latter has, as the name suggests, leaves that are vaguely diamond-shaped in appearance, while *H.* Adam has very small grey and white leaves which are as beautiful in their way as that of any foliage plant. These plants vary considerably and plants with quite large leaves are often sold as being *H.* Adam, but the discerning purchaser should examine them carefully and make a point of selecting the miniature form.

The majority of ivies will branch out quite naturally when the leading growth is pinched out, and, indeed, it is advisable to do this to all that are required to have a full appearance. However *H.* Jubilee is one of the exceptions. When pinched it invariably produces one new stem immediately below the point of severance. And for this simple reason the plant is seldom popular for indoor decoration, since a pleasing shape is just as important as the colouring in many respects.

Another hedera with golden colouring is *H.* Goldchild, a much neater plant, but a little more difficult to care for because of the small amount of chlorophyll in the leaves. Also it is a comparatively new introduction and it will be some time before it can be grown in sufficient quantities to become widely available.

The larger leaved ivies are better where a bolder effect is sought, but all these are vulnerable to red spider mite in hot, dry conditions, so a watch should be kept for their presence. Red spider is often responsible for leaves gradually turning brown and shrivelling from the outer edge; inspection of the undersides should be made when such leaves are noticed. *H. canariensis* (*H.* Gloire de Marengo), *H. maculata* and *H.* Goldleaf are the larger sorts that one is most likely to meet. These are essentially more upright plants and should be grown on canes or against a wall for support.

HELXINE (Baby's Tears or Mind Your Own Business)

Corsica. Hardy. Easy.

On the floor of the damp greenhouse helxine can become a rampant weed, but is not unattractive and has the capacity for smothering any other weeds that may consider setting up home under the greenhouse staging. Besides being weeds they have their uses and can look reasonably attractive as pot plants, and are very little bother. When plants become overgrown it is best policy to replace rather than trim them to shape. Prepare a potful of J.I.P.3 compost, moisten it, then scatter a few trimmings on top – plants will be replaced almost overnight.

HEPTAPLEURUM ARBORICOLA

10 to 18°C. (50 to 65°F.). Easy.

This is something of a miniature schefflera, with similarly shaped leaves that are smaller and more compact. It also branches quite freely when the growing top has been removed, so is better suited to the room where space is limited. Cool conditions are preferred, though it will tolerate higher temperatures without too much discomfort. In good conditions growth is fairly rapid, but this should not create too many problems as the leading shoots can be pinched out at any time to keep the plant within bounds. Good light affording some shelter from the sun is best, and water should be given moderately, particularly in winter. For bolder effect several plants grouped in a container can be pleasing.

HIBISCUS

Tropical Africa. 13 to 18°C. (55 to 65°F.). Easy.

There have been many hybrids of *Hibiscus rosa-sinensis* produced in recent years, many of them really excellent plants that ought to become popular as they become more generally available. There are single and double forms in shades of red, pink, lemon and yellow. Individual flowers last for little more than one day and this, to some, is a disappointment when plants are first purchased. But the disappointment is soon forgotten when it is realised that what flowers may lack in staying power they more than make up for in numbers, as on healthy plants flowers are produced continuously throughout the summer.

Provided a few simple rules are followed these will prove most rewarding plants indoors. Keeping the compost moist is most essential and plants will require to be fed regularly from the

Heptapleurum arboricola

time they are brought indoors. Give them a light position and try to maintain the temperature level indicated above; higher and lower temperatures will do little harm, but by keeping a balanced temperature there will be less likelihood of premature loss of flower buds.

During the winter one can continue to water plants and they will retain their leaves (most of them, anyway!) or they can be dried out and kept in a warm room or garden room until the following early spring, when they can be watered and started into growth again.

Once plants have produced a reasonable amount of new growth in the spring they can be potted into slightly larger pots using J.I.P.3 compost. Plants with single stems can be grown to make attractive standards in about two years. New plants can be obtained from cuttings of new growth in the spring in a temperature of not less than 21°C. (70°F.).

HOSTA (Plantain Lily)

Japan. Hardy. Easy.

With the astonishing increase in the popularity of flower arranging among the ladies hostas have become steadily more important as foliage plants. Foliage is the operative word, as plants are grown, either in the garden or in the garden room, for their attractive leaves, which form the basis of so many flower arrangements. In the garden room they require cool, light conditions and fairly rich compost. Water sparingly during the winter months and more freely while in active growth, when regular feeding will also be necessary. Propagate by dividing clumps in autumn or early spring.

HOYA (Wax Plant)

China, Australia. 13 to 18°C. (55 to 65°F.). Easy.

For best effect these plants should be grown in the garden room with growth twined around overhead wires or trellis framework. The beauty of the exotic, pendulous flowers will then be fully appreciated. Plants may also be grown in pots, but they seldom flower so well as when planted out in the border of the garden room. Keep moist in summer and on the dry side in winter; feed as soon as new growth begins in spring. In good growing conditions plants can be very invasive, so will need hard pruning any time after flowering. Mealy bugs can be troublesome pests should they find their way in between the twining stems of the plant, so a careful watch must be kept in order to eradicate them before

they have a chance to get established. The simplest way to increase plants is to peg shoots into small pots in the form of a layer, cutting them away from the parent plant when they become established.

The variegated form of hoya is less inclined to flower, but is a much more attractive plant and better suited to culture as a conventional house plant. Plants are more attractive if the foliage can be entwined around a framework of some kind. Light conditions are important, and one should never be too heavy-handed with the watering-can, particularly in winter. Propagate from firm cuttings with two leaves and an inch or two of stem pressed firmly into peaty compost.

Grown well in hanging baskets, *Hoya bella*, with its masses of pendulous white flowers tinged with pink, must rank as one of the most exciting of all decorative plants. They will be best suited to the higher temperature mentioned above and must be grown in a raised position in well-drained compost. In lower temperatures plants become hard in appearance and are much less satisfactory.

HYDRANGEA

Japan. Hardy. Easy.

As in the case of *Azalea indica*, the most important requirement of hydrangeas when grown as pot plants is water. They must be kept moist all the time and this usually means a good watering every day, but it is important that the water drains away freely; they should not be allowed actually to stand in water. Purchased in the spring of the year hydrangeas are very little trouble if kept in a light, cool room and watered and fed regularly.

Plants are available in shades of pink, white and blue, and often in less definable shades of mauve. The latter colour is usually the result of the nurseryman having misfired in his treatment of the plant with the chemical alum, which is used to change the colour of pink varieties from their natural pink colouring to blue. If the blueing treatment is not continued each year the plant will slowly revert to its normal pink colour.

After they have finished flowering indoors it is usually best to plant hydrangeas out in the garden where they will quickly establish themselves as colourful shrubs. Before planting it is important that the ground be well watered, as well as the compost in the pot; thereafter the soil surrounding the plant must be kept watered until the plant is established. So many plants fail as a result of the soil drying out after planting. By planting in very acid, peaty soil the

blued varieties will retain their blue colouring; in ordinary soil they will revert to pink. Alternatively, the soil can be treated with alum as required.

Propagate from cuttings taken from blind shoots in March–April and inserted in John Innes cutting compost, or similar, at a temperature in the region of 16°C. (60°F.). Pot on into 5-in. pots as the plants become established and grow on in reasonable warmth until mid-May when they can be placed out of doors for the summer months. Bring indoors, or place in a frost-proof cold frame until the end of the year, when plants can be given extra heat and watered to start them into growth for the new season. While the plants are dormant compost should be kept dry.

HYMENOCALLIS

Tropical America, Guiana. 13 to 18°C. (55 to 65°F.). Moderately easy.

Here we add a touch of luxury by suggesting a plant that is not easy to obtain and will require a fairly high temperature in order to succeed. Belonging to the *Amaryllidaceae* family it has large, strap-like leaves similar to the clivia and white flowers which are absolutely stunning; the scent leaves any perfume coming out of a bottle wondering what it is all about. Even in a large greenhouse it will have the visitor sniffing the atmosphere and enquiring about the pleasant aroma pervading the surroundings.

For plants to retain their rich green appearance it is important that they should be potted on into larger containers at least once a year. There are a number of different sorts available, but preferably one should choose *Hymenocallis ovata*; the flowers are short-lived, but the sheer wonder of them will more than compensate for their brevity.

HYPOCYRTA GLABRA (Clog Plant)

South America. 13 to 16°C. (55 to 60°F.). Easy.

The common name is derived from the interestingly shaped orange flowers that are produced over a long period. An added attraction is the masses of glossy green, oval-shaped leaves that add up to a compact and interesting plant. Given reasonable light and moderate watering they will not prove too difficult. Propagate from top cuttings a few inches in length; remove two or three of the lower leaves and treat in the conventional manner. One cutting in a pot will make some sort of plant, but by inserting five or six in the same pot you will have something much more presentable to show for it in very much less time.

For the garden-room owner these plants will provide an excellent alternative to some of the more usual hanging basket subjects; several plants in a basket produce a better effect. Prune to shape at any time other than when they are in flower.

IMPATIENS (Busy Lizzie)

Tropical Africa. 10 to 16°C. (50 to 60°F.). Easy.

Perhaps because of the amusing common name, or more likely on account of their reasonable price, these are among the most popular of all flowering indoor plants. With good care and regular potting on into slightly larger pots they will attain a height of several feet, but they are usually considered to be compact, low-growing plants. However one should go about caring for them it is essential that they enjoy a light and cool position, moist compost while in active growth, and regular feeding.

Cuttings of non-flowering shoots, or shoots that have had the flowers removed, may be rooted at almost any time; firm cuttings in peaty compost will present no problems if the standard propagating suggestions are followed. Keep a watchful eye for red spider on the underside of leaves and treat accordingly.

IPOMOEA (Morning Glory)

Tropical America. 10 to 16°C. (50 to 60°F.). Easy.

The ordinary morning glory will, of course, grow out of doors during the summer months and tolerate much lower temperatures than those suggested above, but they will do better in the garden room at the slightly higher temperature shown above.

The annuals are very easily raised from seed sown several to a small pot and potted on as required. Provide some support for them to climb the wall and they will certainly provide blue-coloured morning glory flowers throughout the summer.

However, for a change try the perennial greenhouse species and you may well give up the annuals completely. Grown in an arch over the garden room doorway they can be quite spectacular, and when they become overgrown they seem to enjoy being cut back so that they can produce a further flush of new growth and flowers.

IRESINE

Tropical America. 10 to 18°C. (55 to 65°F.). Easy.

Not particularly important plants, the iresines are interesting because of their foliage which is often a deep, blood-red colour. Given reasonable light and standard house plant treatment they are not difficult, and are better grown as fresh plants from cuttings each year – cuttings can be taken at almost any time. The heavier John Innes type compost will be more suitable than the lighter compost advised for the majority of indoor plants.

JASMINE

China. September to February 7 to 13°C. (45 to 55°F.), February to September 13 to 18°C. (55 to 65°F.). Easy.

The tender jasmine is not a particularly interesting pot plant but is, nevertheless, frequently offered for sale during the second two months of the year. No doubt pleasantly scented white flowers help to sell the plant in spite of the fact that they are short-lived. Plants purchased early in the year should be potted on into slightly larger pots as soon as they have finished flowering in order to keep growth active. At the same time a trellis framework of some kind should be provided for new growth to cling to. They may also be planted out in the border in the garden room where prolific growth will be the order of the day. Normally luxuriant growth makes them unsuitable for the small garden room and, even in larger quarters, they will need quite severe and frequent pruning. Plants whose growth is too lush will often produce masses of leaves at the expense of flowers.

KALANCHOË

Tropical Africa. 10 to 18°C. (50 to 65°F.). Easy.

The majority of those that are mass produced are *Kalanchoë* Vulcan which, under natural conditions, is a winter-flowering plant. These are plants, however, that respond to short-day treatment so the nurseryman, by covering them with black polythene and simulating winter day length, can induce plants to flower at almost any time of the year. Indoors they should be kept in light conditions and fed and watered as one would a normal house plant. Flowers and stalks should be completely removed as they die, and the plant potted on into a bigger pot using J.I.P.2 or 3, depending on the size of the plant. Propaga-

Kentia belmoreana

tion may be from cuttings or seed; cuttings should be removed and left for two or three days for the severed end to dry before being inserted in compost.

KENTIA

Lord Howe Islands. 16 to 21°C. (60 to 70°F.). Moderately easy.

Many plants have their names changed, but the nurseryman who is responsible for the production of the vast majority is not always willing to accept the change. The kentia is a good example as we should more properly refer to this elegant palm as a howea. These were popular plants at the turn of the century and have remained in the forefront as desirable indoor plants. Grown from seed sown in moist peat kept at a temperature in the region of 27°C. (80°F.), they take many years to reach maturity, so are expensive plants to purchase. For this reason they are not likely to become best sellers.

When potting on ensure good drainage by putting a layer of crocks in the bottom of the pot, use a rich compost and pot fairly firmly. Although the leaves may seem tough to the touch they are very easily damaged if chemical leaf cleaning agents are used at excessive strength – one should experiment with new cleaning materials before treating the entire plant.

143

LAURUS NOBILIS (Bay Tree)

Southern Europe. Hardy. Easy.

These hardy, evergreen shrubs are much sought after as terrace plants when grown as pyramids, or mop-headed standards. By the time they have reached standard size the plants will be well established in stout tubs and will need regular watering and feeding during the summer months. To prevent scorching of leaves in winter plants should be protected from frost and cold winds. Smaller plants are also occasionally available and should be grown in a cool room where they can have ample light. Scale insects can be troublesome pests, spoiling the appearance of plants, and should be treated with malathion insecticide as soon as noticed.

MARANTA

Tropical America. 13 to 18°C. (55 to 65°F.). Easy and difficult.

Maranta leuconeura erythrophylla has beautifully marked leaves which are a reddish brown in colour. When introduced as a potential house plant some years ago, it gave every indication of being difficult to manage in room conditions. However, this has not proved the case and we find that when grown out of direct sunlight in a moist situation at the temperatures suggested above it can be a most rewarding plant. Moist conditions entail plunging the plant pot in a larger container filled with moist peat or moss. A peaty compost is needed when potting, something akin to that suggested for saintpaulias. Plants will quite happily go for two years without potting on if they are fed with a weak liquid fertiliser while producing new leaves.

M. l. kerchoveana is much better known and has pale green leaves with distinct dark blotches which give it the common name of rabbit's tracks. Another common name is prayer plant, because of the plant's peculiar habit of folding its leaves together like hands in prayer as darkness descends. If these are cared for in the same way as the first-mentioned maranta they should not be too much trouble. Provided a heated propagator is available both can be increased by means of cuttings taken at almost any time; the top section of the plant with some three leaves attached will give the best results.

A number of other marantas may be available and all will require the same conditions and treatment as the two mentioned. One of these is *M. makoyana* (frequently and probably more correctly offered as *Calathea makoyana*) which is very much a plant for the experienced rather than for the beginner. The maximum temperature suggested above will be the most suitable, and moist surroundings for the plant is a must. Even given ideal indoor conditions the leaves of this particular plant will almost inevitably develop brown edges in time. Trimming of these leaves and their eventual removal is the only answer, but there is the compensation that in good

Opposite:
Dieffenbachia Pia, (left), eucalyptus and, in the foreground, *Asplenium nidus*, the bird's nest fern

Maranta leuconeura erythrophylla (left) and *Maranta leuconeura kerchoveana*

conditions new leaves are produced with reasonable freedom during the growing months.

MEDINILLA MAGNIFICA

South East Asia. September to March 16 to 21°C. (60 to 70°F.), April to September 18 to 24°C. (65 to 75°F.). Difficult.

For the garden-room owner who can afford such high temperatures this could well prove to be a most rewarding plant, but it would only lead to frustrating failure if one were to attempt growing them at lower temperatures, particularly in winter. Although the foliage is not particularly attractive, the pendulous pink flowers have show-stopping qualities as the name suggests.

Cuttings are not difficult to root in good heat, prepared from top cuttings with two pairs of leaves attached, or from stem cuttings with one pair of leaves and about 2 in. of stem attached. Start them in peat and pot them on into larger pots as soon as root development demands. In good conditions they will grow into plants 3 or 4 ft. in height reasonably quickly. A few flowers may be produced in the first year, but one usually has to wait for the second year's flowering period to see the plant at its best. Placed with the flowers overhanging a pool feature in the garden room they can be most impressive, and will produce flowers over a period of many months during the summer.

MIMOSA PUDICA (Sensitive Plant)

Tropical America. 13 to 18°C. (55 to 65°F.). Easy.

These are, in fact, perennials, but are best treated as annuals by sowing seed in warm conditions in March and disposing of old plants at the end of the year. The feathery leaves of pale green colour are in themselves attractive, but the principal interest is their sensitive nature which induces them to collapse as if dead at the

Medinilla magnifica

slightest touch. Given light, warmth and standard house plant care they are little bother and will most certainly add interest to one's collection of plants, particularly among younger visitors, who may feel that the plant owner is possessed with some sort of magical touch!

MONSTERA (Swiss Cheese Plant)

Tropical America. 13 to 18°C. (55 to 65°F.). Easy.

Universally this must surely rate as one of the most popular of all indoor plants, a popularity that never seems to wane. It has all the necessary characteristics: easy to care for, naturally glossy leaves that are serrated and in time perforated, and rather weird and exotic aerial roots.

Place out of direct sunlight, keep the compost moist without ever allowing it to remain saturated for long periods, and feed regularly during the spring and summer months. Leaves will be improved by periodic cleaning with a soft sponge, using either water or one of the proprietary leaf-cleaning agents. Avoid using chemicals too frequently and at all costs ensure that soft new leaves at the top of the plant are not treated, as they are very easily damaged. Irreparable damage may also be caused to young leaves by handling them before they unfold. When the compost in the pot becomes too wet plants will sometimes exude droplets of water from the edges of leaves, an indication that the amount of water given should be reduced. The aerial roots present problems and one is often advised that these should be removed. Unless there is an excessive number of roots it is far better to direct the tips into the soil when they are long enough, and to tie the roots in to the stem of the plant to keep them tidy.

Some years ago, in the home of a friend, I was intrigued to see the root of a monstera growing over the side of a floor-level container and disappearing under the carpet. Tracing the root, which looked like an electrical cable, I was amazed to see that it had travelled fully 12 ft. across the room and was making its way along the wall underneath the carpet – some wag suggested that it was on its way to the pantry!

In commercial establishments new plants are raised with little bother from seed; they may also be raised from cuttings, but seed will give much more attractive plants for room decoration. When potting it is necessary to use a peaty mixture.

Besides the *Monstera deliciosa* (syn. *Philodendron pertusum*) described above there is another, *M. pertusa borsigiana*, which has much smaller leaves and more upright habit of growth,

Foliage of *Mimosa pudica*

Bottom: Fruit and inflorescence of *Monstera deliciosa*

and is preferred where space is limited. Both plants will produce arum-type flowers when they are a few years old; these have an exotic attraction and remain colourful for about four days. Flowers are later followed by the fruit which is edible and must be left on the plant to become thoroughly ripe before eating. In Australia one of the common names is fruit salad plant because the fruit has all the flavours of a fruit salad. However, it must be admitted that the fruit does not look particularly appetising when it has ripened.

NEANTHE BELLA (Parlour Palm)

Mexico. 13 to 18°C. (55 to 65°F.). Easy.

More correctly *Chamaedorea elegans bella*, it is not difficult to understand why the nurseryman prefers the simpler name when offering this plant for sale. Compact and attractive, these palms are especially well suited to the plant

grower who has limited space. They are also much favoured as plants for use in bottle gardens as they are also slow growing. Provided plants are grown in an open, free-draining compost at regulated temperature in light surroundings they are likely to remain attractive for many years with little attention. Browning of leaf tips is one of the few problems and is usually caused by wet and cold conditions.

NERINE BOWDENII

South Africa. Hardy. Easy.

There are a number of hybrids now becoming available. All of them are easy to manage and may be planted out of doors in sheltered areas, and they are particularly attractive when seen at the base of a wall where they can enjoy full sun. As trouble-free pot plants they remain dormant from May to September when they require no water and may be tucked away on a high shelf in

Nerine bowdenii

the garden room where they can get plenty of sunlight. As soon as flower spikes appear watering should be started, but must at no time be excessive.

When potting use J.I.P.2 compost and ensure that pots are well drained. For best effect up to five bulbs should be planted in a 5-in. pot; bulbs are planted to about half their depth. Small offsets from the main bulbs are the best means of propagation, but if one has patience they may also be raised from seed. In later summer nerines are especially fine as temporary and colourful room plants.

NEOREGELIA CAROLINAE TRICOLOR

Tropical South America. 16 to 21°C. (60 to 70°F.). Easy.

In this section of the bromeliad family one is likely to come across a number of other neoregelias, but the plant mentioned in the heading is by far the most popular. Colourful leaves are arranged in a flat rosette that form a typical watertight urn which must be kept filled with water at all times. Cream and pink variegated leaves will remain much more attractive if the plant is given good light in which to grow, but very hot sun must be guarded against. As the plant matures and is about to flower the shorter leaves in the centre of the rosette change colour to a brilliant red, giving it a most striking appearance.

The small blue flowers produced remain more or less at water level in the urn and are not so attractive, but the plant itself will more than compensate for the poor show of flower. The main rosette gradually dies off after the plant has flowered and new plants are made from the shoots which appear close to the base of the parent stem.

For general cultivation one should follow the information given for the aechmea on page 76. For propagation, see also page 54.

Neoregelia carolinae tricolor

NEPHTHYTIS EMERALD GEM

Mexico. 16 to 21°C. (60 to 70°F.). Moderately easy.

There are any number of inferior types of this particular variety available but, if there is a choice, those with pale grey-green foliage should be selected as they make much the most superior plants. If the recommended temperature is provided they are not especially difficult, but in low temperatures success is all but impossible. Light shade, moist surroundings and a peaty compost would be other recommendations, also weak liquid fertiliser while they are growing. Propagate from top cuttings about 6 in. in length with two or three firm leaves attached.

NERIUM OLEANDER

Japan. October to April 7 to 13°C. (45 to 55°F.), April to October 13 to 18°C. (55 to 65°F.). Easy.

Oleanders are the sort of plants that go on for many years once they have been acquired and are little trouble, though space demanding. Grow in good light and water freely during the summer months, reducing the amount in the autumn and keeping plants nearly dry during the winter. After flowering, shoots of the previous year's growth should be cut down to about 6 in. from their base, and any growths that appear at the base of the flower trusses should be removed as soon as they are seen. Propagate from cuttings about 5 in. in length taken in late spring.

In summer oleanders make fine terrace plants; for this purpose they are best in large pots or wooden tubs. Regular feeding will be necessary once plants have been potted up in these larger containers.

PACHYSTACHYS LUTEA (Lollipop Plant)

Tropical South America. 13 to 18°C. (55 to 65°F.). Difficult.

At the time of writing this plant is enjoying a short burst of popularity, and time will best indicate whether or not it has managed to stay the course. Susceptibility to whitefly attack may well be one reason for the pachystachys not attaining the popularity that the attractive yellow bracts deserve. Bracts are a paler yellow in colour compared to the aphelandra which this plant resembles, but the plain green leaves do not have such attractive markings and one cannot imagine the day when the aphelandra will take second place. The bracts, produced in greater quantity than on the aphelandra, bear a marked resemblance to a child's well-sucked lollipop.

A light window is required indoors, or a lightly shaded position in the garden room, and the temperature needs to be in the region of 16°C. (60°F.). Keep well fed and well watered; any drying out will quickly result in the plants flagging and in time shedding their lower leaves. Most important, however, is to keep a watchful eye for whitefly on the undersides of the leaves and to take precautions as soon as they are noticed. The best method of increasing plants is by means of cuttings taken with a pair of leaves and a piece of stem; given reasonable treatment and conditions they root very easily.

PANDANUS (Screw Pine)

South East Asia. Minimum 16°C. (60°F.). Easy.

The cream and green, or white and green, leaves of the pandanus radiate from a central stem, and when well cared for may attain a length in excess of 8 ft. when the roots are confined to large pots. One should not, however, expect such magnificent leaves in the home; indoors 3 or 4 ft. would be the expected maximum. It must also be said that one would indeed be lucky to acquire any sort of pandanus plant, as they seem to be forever in short supply. This is mainly because new plants are propagated from young plantlets growing up from the base of the parent stem, and these are seldom very plentiful. These plants abhor crowding and show off their true grandure when grown as individual specimens with ample space to spread their magnificent leaves.

Good light is important, but care must be taken not to overwater the compost during the winter months. Annual potting on is recommended, otherwise roots find their way out through the bottom of the pot to the detriment of the plant.

PASSIFLORA (Passion Flower)

Tropical America. October to April 7 to 13°C. (45 to 55°F.), April to October 13 to 18°C. (55 to 65°F.). Easy.

Passiflora caerulea is the variety most likely to be encountered; it is hardy in sheltered areas, but will do better in a garden room or home where reasonable warmth can be provided. In good conditions growth can become almost rampant, so a reasonable amount of trellis or framework should be prepared to support the new growth. In the garden room pleasant shade will be provided if this plant is allowed to grow through a wire framework suspended a few feet above head level. Plants are much more floriferous if the roots can be confined to a small pot and, if planted in the border of the garden room, the pot is plunged in the soil in the border. When treated in this way it is of the utmost importance that watering should not be neglected, especially in hot weather.

PELARGONIUM

South Africa.

Here we have a vast range of plants suitable for indoor and garden room decoration and for the garden display in summer. Almost all are easy to grow if they have a light position and one is not too heavy-handed with the watering-can.

All of those suitable for pot culture can be raised from cuttings taken in autumn or spring, though autumn cuttings taken after plants have flowered is advised as they get off to a much better start for the new season. Cuttings about 4 in. in length should be removed and allowed to dry for twenty four hours before they are inserted in sandy compost.

Plants of considerable size can be grown by keeping them over the years, but they usually flower much more satisfactorily if raised anew each year. Even so, many of those referred to as geraniums and used extensively for summer bedding can be induced to climb the garden-room wall to a height of 6 to 8 ft. to give a colourful summer display.

The ivy-leaved sorts are excellent for hanging baskets and very little trouble to care for. There are also those with scented leaves which are a pleasant novelty, but require rather too much space for the comparatively poor display they give.

Pachystachys lutea

Peperomia magnoliaefolia

PELLIONIA DAVEAUANA

South East Asia. Minimum 13°C. (55°F.). Easy.

Given warm conditions in which to grow, this plant will develop at quite a rapid pace, particularly so if the roots which form along the stem are allowed to penetrate into moist gravel or peat. Essentially trailing or creeping plants, they are suited to growing in pots indoors or in hanging baskets or planted in borders in the garden room. When in baskets the longer growth should be pinned in under the basket to give a more finished effect; it will also be important to ensure that water is given regularly. A peaty compost is needed, and to increase plants it is a simple matter to remove pieces a few inches in length which have rooted into the staging. Alternatively, pieces may be pegged down in small pots and severed from the main stem of the plant when they have obviously rooted – a relatively quick process.

PEPEROMIA

Tropical America. Minimum 13°C. (55°F.). Easy.

All reasonably compact plants, the peperomias will do fairly well at temperatures less than that suggested above, but for best results a minimum of 13°C. (55°F.) should be maintained. Provide a light position out of strong sunlight, and err on the side of dryness when watering, as soggy conditions result in tired, limp plants. For the indoor gardener with an artistic turn of mind who enjoys arranging mixed plants in containers the peperomias can be quite an asset, as they are all of a reasonably neutral colour and take up little space. With house plants likely to remain in the same pot for twelve months or more it is advisable to use a loam-based potting compost when transferring plants from one container to another. However, the peperomias are the exception to the rule and much prefer the soilless composts.

Of those offered for sale *Peperomia magnoliae-folia* is probably the best known. It has stiff leaves with cream and green variegation compactly arranged on short, stout stems. Similar in colour *P. glabella variegata* is of natural trailing habit, and to keep in good shape requires to be renewed regularly by propagating easily rooted cuttings a few inches in length.

P. caperata is a delightful little plant with dark green crinkled leaves which form into compact cushions of growth on the top of the soil. These can be propagated quite easily from individual leaves pressed into peaty compost just far enough for them to remain erect; they are prepared and treated in very much the same way as leaf cuttings of saintpaulia. There is also a much more rare variegated form with smaller leaves coloured pale green and cream. These are not so plentiful as propagating material is much less easy to obtain; cuttings taken from individual leaves merely produce green plants, so in order to get the more attractive variegation cuttings must be prepared with part of the main stem of the plant attached.

The grey-leaved *P. hederaefolia* should be treated in exactly the same way as *caperata*, both in respect of culture and propagation.

PHILODENDRON

Tropical America. Minimum 13°C. (55°F.). Moderately easy.

These members of the *Araceae* family provide us with many fine green plants with leaves of an infinite variety of shapes much sought after by those wanting plants with an architectural appearance. There are some variegated forms, but they seldom do as well as the naturally coloured. Being indigenous to the tropical jungles of South America, they will all be the better for growing in an atmosphere as moist and humid as possible, where for preference the temperature should be in the region of 18°C. (65°F.). Most will tolerate temperatures as low as the 13°C. given above provided plants are kept on the dry side and lower temperatures apply for only short periods. Some years ago we were amazed to find that during a particularly cold winter *Philodendron bipinnatifidum* survived in temperatures that dropped as low as freezing point; compost was kept very much on the dry side. However, one would not recommend such low temperatures as the plants will just about survive and take a considerable time to recover.

A moist atmosphere surrounding the plants is essential if they are to prosper indoors or in the greenhouse, so it is wise to provide a bed of moist peat in which the pots can be plunged to their rims. Many of the plants will produce aerial roots which will find their way into the peat and provide an additional source of moisture. A position out of direct sunlight is also needed if leaves are to retain their rich green colouring and not take on a hard yellow appearance. The majority can be raised from seed sown in moist peat in a very warm temperature somewhere in the region of 27°C. (80°F.), but it will be easier to propagate the smaller leaved ones from cuttings raised in warm, moist conditions.

P. bipinnatifidum has a name which is rather off-putting, but it is a very fine plant for an area that can offer ample space for the large, deeply cut leaves that radiate from the centre of the pot. These are superb plants when placed as individual specimens on a pedestal of some kind, and will in time develop short, stout trunks that can be particularly attractive when older leaves die naturally and are removed from the lower part of the plant.

P. elegans is not an easy plant either to grow or acquire but, as the name suggests, it is one of the most attractive of the purely green plants. Being of a naturally climbing habit it will do very much better if a mossed support can be provided into which the aerial roots can find their way; it is essential that the moss be kept moist. Do this by spraying regularly, or by leaning the plant over and watering the support more heavily with a watering-can – if the plant is not tilted the surplus water will run into the compost and make it much too wet. The aim when watering should be to keep the compost moist, but not permanently saturated.

P. hastatum and *P. Tuxla* are very similar in appearance, both having stout climbing stems to which arrow-shaped leaves are attached by strong petioles which may be anything up to 2 ft. in length on more mature plants. Where a jungle effect in a large garden room is contemplated this would seem to be an essential plant for forming part of the background. Treat in almost exactly the same way as the *P. elegans* previously mentioned.

P. laciniatum has smaller leaves and hairy stems and leaf stalks, and will develop into a plant of considerable size in time, but it is important when preparing larger specimens to ensure that several small plants are potted in the larger pot in order to provide a plant of reasonable fullness. Although it is quite quick growing in good conditions it need not be allowed to push one out of house and home, as unwanted growth can be cut away at any time.

P. melanochrysum is quite different from the majority of philodendrons in that the leaves have a dark, almost velvety appearance instead of the more usual glossy green. They are also smaller than those of any previously mentioned, and can be guaranteed to attract attention in almost any grouping of plants, however exotic the others may be. A moist support and warm conditions is again advised as this species is inclined to be a little temperamental if conditions are not to its liking.

P. scandens has a quality which the most successful of pop stars could well envy, for it has been in the top twenty house plants for more years than most of us in the business care to remember. The common name of sweetheart plant probably helps; the name is derived from the heart-like shape of the green leaf. It is also one of the easiest of plants to care for indoors, another obvious reason for its popularity. It will tolerate much less agreeable conditions than the majority of philodendrons, but like all these plants the better the conditions the better the plant will respond. It will certainly do better in moist conditions at a temperature in the region of 18°C. (65°F.) than it will in a dry environment at lower temperatures.

P. wendlandii is one of my favourites, and the shuttlecock formation of the leaves is quite different to that of any of the other philodendrons mentioned here. Leaves are compactly arranged and radiate in stiff, upright fashion from the centre of the plant in much the same way as those of the bird's nest fern (*Asplenium nidus*). Scarcity of stock is another problem here, but plants are worth acquiring if the required conditions can be provided. The appearance of this plant will be greatly enhanced if the leaves are cleaned periodically with a moist sponge. All the philodendrons will benefit from this sort of treatment, except those which do not have glossy leaves, such as *P. melanochrysum*.

PHOENIX

South East Asia, Africa. September to April 13 to 18°C. (55 to 65°F.), April to September 18 to 24°C. (65 to 75°F.). Moderately easy.

Growing feather palms to a reasonable size is a long, slow process, so plants of specimen size are invariably expensive. The plants require a warm, light position in which to grow, preferably in a moist atmosphere. Water freely during the spring and summer months, and in moderation at other times. In the garden room, and indoors where it is practical, plants will benefit from having their leaves syringed with water during the summer months. Iron deficiency is a problem that will result in leaves taking on a hard, yellow appearance; sequestrene of iron used according

to the manufacturer's directions will help to combat this. With larger plants an old remedy was to place a piece of sulphate of iron on top of the soil, a little of which was watered into the compost in sufficient quantity to keep the plant in good condition.

One of the most graceful of the feather palms is *Phoenix roebelinii*, which has delicate leaves that appear almost silver when the light catches them at the right angle. *P. canariensis* is a little coarser in appearance, and develops into a very much larger plant in time. The date palm of commerce is *P. dactylifera*. All may be grown from seed sown early in the year in a mixture of peat and sand; a high minimum temperature of not less than 24°C. (75°F.) should be maintained.

PILEA

Tropical America. 13 to 18°C. (55 to 65°F.). Easy.

On the whole pileas are small, compact plants which will all benefit from having their growing tips removed periodically in order to induce a more bushy appearance. They are also what we might term expendable plants, in that it is often better to make new plants every year or so and dispose of the older parents which lose their shape and attraction if kept for too long. Cuttings a few inches in length root very easily in standard house plant compost if placed in a warm propa-

gating unit, several cuttings to each pot. When they have rooted and obviously begun to grow the growing points of each cutting should be removed. Grown in moderate light in a warm place they will give little trouble. Feed with a weak liquid fertiliser while in active growth.

The silvery grey *Pilea cadierei* was at one time the most popular but has now been superseded by the much more compact and attractive *P. c. nana*, which has smaller leaves of brighter appearance. The artillery plant, *P. microphylla*, gets its common name from the way seed pods 'explode' and scatter seed in all directions; other than this interesting facility it would seem to have little to recommend it for house decoration. There are a number of other pileas that one is likely to come across, the majority of them being reasonably easy to manage, but by far the best introduction has been *P. repens*, better known as *P.* Moon Valley, which is a really superb little plant, very easy to manage.

PITTOSPORUM

Australia, New Zealand, Japan. October to April 7 to 10°C. (45 to 50°F.), April to October 13 to 18°C. (55 to 65°F.). Easy.

Many of these are grown purely for their foliage which is used extensively by florists in flower designs. They are, however, occasionally made available as pot plants and can be very effective when grown in a cool, light garden room or

greenhouse. There are a number of different sorts available with green and variegated leaves. *Pittosporum tenuifolium* has glossy green leaves with wavy margins and darker coloured stems. It is the hardiest and the most popular. Some have fragrant flowers which are interesting, but not particularly attractive. Prune to shape after flowering, and propagate new plants from pieces 4 to 5 in. in length inserted in sandy compost in summer.

PLATYCERIUM ALCICORNE (Stag's Horn Fern)

**Australia. Minimum 16°C. (60°F.).
Moderately easy.**

There are a number of platyceriums available, but this is the one most likely to be encountered. All require similar conditions in which to grow, and the emphasis should be on moisture and warmth. Plants will do quite well in the 16°C. (60°F.) minimum suggested, but will thrive that much better if the temperature can be kept at a higher level. It is important to remember, though, that hot and dry conditions can do more harm than good, so increased temperatures should also call for increased humidity.

Platyceriums can be used in a number of ways: as conventional pot plants, attached to pieces of bark or wood or, better still, several plants can be grouped together in a hanging basket. Simple wire baskets are by far the best and should be lined with sphagnum moss (not polythene, which is often used today) before being filled with a peaty compost. Plant at least four around the edge of the basket and give the compost a good watering. For the first few months the basket should be placed in a large flower pot at waist level in the garden room or greenhouse, so that a watchful eye can be kept on it in the early stages before it is suspended overhead. By using moss as a lining the anchor leaves of the plant will in time completely cover the basket while the antler-shaped leaves will spear out in all directions, creating a quite dramatic effect.

Another method of setting off the leaves to best advantage is to attach young plants to flat pieces of wood or bark, using moss and plastic-covered wire, and hanging them on the wall of the garden room, or indoors. If displayed in this way it is important that the plants should be plunged in a bucket of water at least once each week. Attempting to water them by spraying over the moss will be quite futile.

PLEOMELE REFLEXA

**India, Ceylon. 13 to 18°C. (55 to 65°F.).
Moderately easy.**

Superb plants that are painfully slow growing and, consequently, in short supply. Nevertheless they are worth acquiring for their attractive golden yellow foliage. They require good light, 157

compost that is never too wet and potting on into J.I.P.3 compost when the pots are well filled with roots. Wet and cold winter conditions can be particularly harmful.

PLUMBAGO

South Africa. September to April 7 to 13°C. (45 to 55°F.) April to September 13 to 18°C. (55 to 65°F.). Easy.

In the garden room or greenhouse there can be few climbing plants more colourful and effective than *Plumbago capensis* with its cascading pale blue flowers. There is also a white form, *P. c. alba*.

Plants may be grown in large pots with the growth trained on tall bamboo canes, but they seem much happier and give an infinitely more impressive show if planted in a border of good compost in the garden room with the growth spread out on a wall trellis. Plants may be raised from seed sown in February, or from cuttings 3 in. in length taken at any time during the summer months. Before planting out in the border it is better to allow the plants to become well established in 5-in. pots first. They will then grow away much more readily. Water should be given freely during the summer months, reducing the amount in October and

November, then give the bare minimum until new growth begins. After flowering, shoots should be pruned back to 2 or 3 in. from their base.

PODOCARPUS MACROPHYLLUS

China, Japan. 10 to 13°C. (50 to 60°F.). Easy.

Substantial trees in their native habitat, podo-carpus also make attractive potted plants and are particularly effective when the pale green new growth is set off against darker, more mature foliage.

Pot them on annually, using J.I.P.3 compost, until plants are eventually in 10-in. sized pots or small tubs, where they can then be maintained by regular feeding.

POINSETTIA (Christmas Flower)

Mexico. 16 to 18°C. (60 to 65°F.). Moderately easy.

The botanists are forever telling us plant producers that we should refer to crotons as codiaeums, *Aralia elegantissima* as *Dizygotheca elegantissima* and the poinsettia as *Euphorbia pulcherrima*. Admittedly, we should comply with their wishes, but at the same time we have to sell our plants and a very difficult tongue-twisting name merely results in sales resistance. The average Mrs Jones is our most important customer, and poinsettia rolls easily off her tongue, but *Euphorbia pulcherrima* is a very different matter. And so we continue to favour the simpler name.

Some fifteen years ago I was entrusted with the task of caring for the small poinsettia crop on a large nursery and found the task a most onerous one. In those days poinsettias were tender to the point whereby an inadvertent sneeze in their presence seemed sufficient reason for them to drop their leaves almost on the instant. At the same time also, plants seemed to grow as you looked at them and very rapidly were capable of achieving an unwieldy height of 5 or 6 ft.

In the mid-sixties, however, we saw a quite remarkable change when plants which appeared to have a built-in resistance to disease and leaf drop arrived on the scene. Almost simultaneously the near magical effects of growth retarders were beginning to show their potential.

The hardier *Euphorbia mikkelsen* plants came from America, as did all the more tender ones previously, and were infinitely easier for the nurseryman to care for, temperature and watering requirements being much less critical. This meant that they were much simpler for the householder to manage indoors. It became quite common for us to receive complimentary letters concerning poinsettia plants purchased at Christmas which had remained in colourful condition for six months or more.

Plants are available in three colours, white, pink and red, although the latter is by far the most popular. The colourful part of the plant is known as a bract and, in fact, consists of coloured leaves – the actual flowers are short-lived and comparatively insignificant.

A further improvement in the poinsettia has been due to the introduction of varieties, such as *E*. Mikkelrochford and *E.* Annette Hegg, which produce anything up to ten evenly branched sideshoots when the leading growth is removed. In the past it was necessary to insert three cuttings in a 5-in. pot in order to get a plant of reasonable size, but now one pinched cutting will produce several growths and a mass of coloured bracts.

Of the chemicals used for restricting the height of poinsettias Cycocel is probably the most used. Plants so treated have internodes of little more than 1 in. in length, whereas untreated plants will develop stems as much as 6 in. in length between each leaf. Besides getting many more leaves to a given height, the advantages in respect of moving and packing plants so treated is quite

Plumbago capensis

considerable. Plants soon grow out of the effects of growth retarding chemicals and early potted plants need two or three treatments. This is one reason why plants kept from one year to the next indoors will grow to be very much taller than the plant originally purchased.

Indoors, poinsettia plants require to be grown in a light, sunny window at the temperature suggested above, and water should be given as plants require it and not for the sake of giving it. Waterlogged conditions will quickly result in yellowing and loss of lower leaves. In time yellowing and loss of leaves will be quite natural to the plant, and is soon followed by the loss of the bracts. As this natural process takes place the amount of water should be gradually reduced until the compost is almost dry. The stems of the plant should then be cut back to about 4 in. in length and the compost kept just moist. The plant must then be stored in a warm, dry place until new growth is seen, when watering can be gradually restarted. When the plant has become reasonably established it can be potted on into a slightly larger container using J.I.P.2 compost. As growth gets under way the top 4 in. of each stem can be removed and inserted in peaty compost at a temperature of some 18°C. (65°F.) in order to produce fresh plants.

With these superior varieties keeping plants indoors from one year to the next is not so 159

Opposite: Shown along the back, from left to right, are *Impatiens petersiana*, *Gynura sarmentosa*, *Beloperone guttata*, the shrimp plant, and *Stephanotis floribunda*. In front, again from left to right, are *Tradescantia bicolor*, *Peperomia magnoliaefolia*, and the variegated ice plant, *Sedum sieboldii medio-variegatum*

difficult, but getting the same plants to produce flowering bracts for a second time in the home is a different matter and considered by some to be quite impossible. However, our correspondence suggests that this is not so and many enthusiasts do, in fact, succeed. Whatever else may be done to encourage bracts for a second time there is one absolute essential, and that is that plants should be subjected only to natural daylight from mid-September until their natural flowering time in December. Flowers initiate and develop according to the amount of light available, and any additional artificial light in the evening will merely result in production of additional leaves at the expense of flowers.

When caring for plants indoors it is important to ensure that water is not allowed to get onto leaves when the weather is cold and temperatures are likely to be inadequate. Bracts can be easily damaged in this way.

POLYSCIAS

Pacific Islands. 13 to 18°C. (55 to 65°F.). Moderately easy.

The keen plantsman is likely to encounter a number of polyscias, which belong to the *Araliaceae* family. All these are better suited to greenhouse cultivation rather than indoors, so the garden room is a possibility. *Polyscias balfouriana*, and in particular the improved form *P. b.* Pinocchio, is one of the best, the improved form having creamy-yellow leaves. In time it will attain a height of 10 ft. or more when confined to a pot, but this will take a number of years. Fresh plants may be raised from top cuttings 6 in. in length inserted in a warm propagator at almost any time of the year other than in the depth of winter. Water freely when in active growth and moderately at other times; if suggested temperatures cannot be maintained during the winter months plants will fare better if the compost is kept on the dry side. This advice applies to almost all plants grown in the greenhouse, garden room or indoors.

PRIMULA

China. 10 to 13°C. (50 to 55°F.). Easy.

Nurserymen raise primulas from seed by the million annually. The principal varieties for pot culture are *Primula sinensis*, *P. acaulis*, *P. obconica* and *P. malacoides*. In recent years we have seen a vast increase in the number of *P. acaulis* available. As a greenhouse is normally required for seed raising and every seed packet gives full instructions, it seems pointless to consider this side

of their culture here. The house owner is more concerned with the care of established plants once they have been purchased.

The primulas mentioned here will all require cool, light and moist conditions in which to grow. Having flowered indoors the *acaulis* varieties can be planted out in the garden in a moist, shaded position, but the others should be discarded when no longer attractive.

PUNICA (Pomegranate)

Persia. 10 to 16°C. (50 to 60°F.). Easy.

These plants are raised from seed sown in a high temperature in spring, or from cuttings a few inches in length taken at the same time and inserted in peaty compost. Keep moist in summer and a little on the dry side in winter, and grow in reasonable light. Almost anything that will produce fruit when grown as a pot plant has a fascination for a great many gardeners and the pomegranate is no exception. But, like many other fruits grown in pots, this one is not particularly exciting, as the fruits generally remain quite small and more often than not will split their outer skins before they have ripened properly. Nevertheless, it is quite an attractive plant whose colourful orange flowers are often confused with those of the fuchsia when seen for the first time.

RHIPSALIS

Tropical America, Africa. 13 to 18°C. (55 to 65°F.). Easy.

These tropical forest plants require a warm, humid atmosphere, but should not be too wet at their roots, so a well-drained compost is essential. To encourage drainage a 2-in. layer of crocks should be placed in the bottom of the pot before introducing the compost, which should be of a peaty nature. Small, star-shaped flowers are produced in profusion in winter, and there are numerous colours, of which the rose pink is probably best. New plants may be raised from seed sown in good heat in March, or by means of cuttings which root very easily at almost any time of the year if reasonable heat is available, somewhere in the order of 21°C. (70°F.).

RHOEO DISCOLOR (Three Men in a Boat)

Mexico. 13 to 18°C. (55 to 65°F.). Moderately easy.

One of the more aristocratic members of the tradescantia family (*Commelinaceae*), the rhoeo

has stiff, upright leaves streaked with pale yellow markings, the undersides of which have a purple hue. Flowers are borne low down at the base of the leaves and are an unusual boat shape in appearance, but are otherwise undistinguished. The common name is derived from the shape of the flower which is said to resemble three men in a boat.

Although belonging to the tradescantias, the rhoeo will require much more humid and agreeable conditions; if the minimum temperature suggested cannot be maintained then they are not worth attempting. Propagation is best effected by removing and planting up individually the offshoots which are in time produced at the base of healthy plants.

RHOICISSUS RHOMBOIDEA

Natal. October to April 7 to 13°C. (45 to 55°F.), April to October 13 to 18°C. (55 to 65°F.). Easy.

One of the toughest of all the house plants, *Rhoicissus rhomboidea*, the grape ivy, is a tendril climber with glossy green leaves. With adequate watering and feeding it will thrive in warm, airy conditions, and will withstand the dry heat of central heating more readily than the other vine, *Cissus antarctica*. Given the support of canes or trellis and placed in a favourable position the young growth will romp away and will need pruning back periodically to keep the plant in shape. Cuttings with two leaves on the stem taken about half an inch below the lower leaf joint will root easily.

RICINUS COMMUNIS (Castor Oil Plant)

Tropical Africa. 10 to 13°C. (50 to 55°F.). Easy.

The large leaves of *Ricinus communis* are similar to those of *Aralia sieboldii*, which is often known as the castor oil plant as well, but they are of a more purplish tinge and grow more freely. These are annuals which are grown from seed sown in the spring. The seeds ought to be soaked in water for several hours to soften them before sowing.

Pot them on as soon as necessary, and in a comparatively short space of time handsome plants will be produced. Keep well watered and fed and place them in a good light to get the best out of them.

Besides being useful indoor plants they are equally attractive when hardened off and planted out in the garden in the centre of wide beds of annual flowers.

SAINTPAULIA (African Violet)

Tropical Africa. 16 to 21°C. (60 to 70°F.). Moderately easy.

This must surely be the most popular flowering pot plant in the world today. The poinsettia and pot chrysanthemum growers may dispute this statement, but when you consider the vast numbers of African violets which are produced in small pots throughout the year there seems little doubt that they are miles ahead of the poinsettias and chrysanthemums which demand much larger pots as a rule, and so require very much more greenhouse space than the saintpaulia in which to grow.

Only a few years ago the very suggestion that saintpaulias could be termed moderately easy to grow would have been laughed at. But in the past few years there has been a marked change in their ability to withstand the vicissitudes of the average living room. One has only to stand at a major flower show such as Chelsea and listen to the comments of visitors to realise that the saintpaulia is losing much of its tender, almost impossible image.

How do we account for this? Obviously modern homes are better lit, better heated and, most important of all, the householder is acquiring a great deal more knowledge and skill in indoor plant care. However, the real reason for the improvement lies with one or two of the German nurserymen (Holtkamp and Englert in particular) who have spent many years on the development of more durable strains of saintpaulia, their Rhapsodie and Diana strains being among the best available today. In the past the tendency among hybridists has seemed to be towards the production of plants with an ever-increasing range of flower colours and shapes, with not much thought to the constitutional qualities. This has changed in recent years and Holtkamp and Englert, like Mikkelsen with his tougher American poinsettia, have now produced plants which appear to have a built-in tolerance of difficult conditions. Having done this they are now turning out plants with a better range of colours which still retain the quality of durability.

Another considerable step has been the development of plants with non-dropping flowers; this, in fact, means that when a flower dies it still remains attached to the flower stalk instead of dropping off amongst the leaves where it would rot and cause all sorts of fungus problems. Hygiene plays a very important part in the care of saintpaulias; any dead matter in the way of flowers, leaves or leaf stalks should be removed as soon as it is seen. Incidentally, all these newer saintpaulias are protected by licence

Opposite: *Ricinis communis*, the castor oil plant

163

A popular plant at Christmas time with its showy bracts in full display is the poinsettia, *Euphorbia pulcherrima*

Sansevieria trifasciata
Golden Hahnii and
S. t. Hahnii

and royalties have to be paid for all cuttings that may be propagated in any quantity.

It has been my contention for many years that the most important single requirement for the successful growing of saintpaulias indoors is adequate light. A sunny window-sill, with protection from strong, direct sunlight only, is the ideal position, and the kitchen window-sill for preference as there is usually less curtaining, so more light there. Though the average saintpaulia grower usually hesitates to expose his plants to full sunlight, he may take comfort, as I did, from the following quotation from a letter from a saintpaulia grower in Portugal. 'It makes very good strong plants, but wants to be in the house, on a sunny window-sill, with as much light and sun as possible, even the scorching Portuguese summer sun.'

When growing plants on a sunny window-sill it is of the utmost importance that plants should only be watered from below, as any water on the leaves or flowers will quickly result in scorch marks and other damage when exposed to full sunlight. Actually, watering from the bottom by placing plants in a saucer of water and allowing

them to drink up what is required should become standard practice indoors. It is also advisable to use tepid water, as very cold water can be particularly harmful.

Other than light and proper watering, adequate temperature is also of considerable importance and one should endeavour to maintain an even temperature in the region of 18°C. (65°F.). Wildly fluctuating temperatures will be more harmful than temperature that is constant but slightly below that advised. During the spring and summer months it is also necessary to feed plants regularly with a weak liquid fertiliser; weak and often is much more preferable than occasional heavy doses.

Growing plants of reasonable quality presents few problems to many saintpaulia owners, but they are often perplexed by the fact that otherwise healthy plants are reluctant to flower. Much of this is due to the fact that most fertilisers manufactured for indoor plants contain a very high level of nitrogen in their make up, and foliage plants do particularly well on such a diet. Flowering plants, however, require a fertiliser with a higher phosphate content if they are to flower well. A word in the ear of the garden sundriesman is the best advice; he will be able to recommend a suitable product.

Few plants do well in pots that are out of proportion to their size, and the saintpaulia is no exception. Many flowering plants, in fact, flower better when their roots are confined to a smaller area. Potting on into larger containers is only necessary about every second year, but this may be required more frequently in the case of vigorous plants. When potting, it is better to use half-pots rather than pots of full depth as the plants will root more freely and the squat saintpaulia will look more attractive in the shallow pot. Do the potting in the spring of the year and use a compost composed of equal parts J.I.P.2 and fresh sphagnum peat. After potting, the compost should have a good watering and thereafter be kept on the dry side for five or six weeks to encourage the roots to search actively for moisture, resulting in a better root system. With all pot plants a healthy root system is the basis of good culture. The grower of a few plants may feel it is harsh treatment, but it will help considerably towards building up stronger plants if the flowers are removed from young plants and from those which are newly potted. By doing this the plant will not have to expend energy on the production of flowers, and much healthier and more prolific leaf development will result.

A rule-of-thumb tip for watering is that the leaves should be just perceptibly allowed to droop, or become slightly limp to the touch, between each application of water.

SANSEVIERIA (Mother-in-law's Tongue)

Tropical Africa. Minimum 10°C. (50°F.). Easy.

Far and away the most important member of this family where house plants are concerned is *Sansevieria trifasciata laurentii*, which has the amusing common name of mother-in-law's tongue. Numerous reasons are put forward for the plant having acquired such a name, one of them being that, like mothers-in-law, once you have got one of these plants you never seem to be able to get rid of it! And, with reasonable care, it does seem to be almost indestructible, and to almost thrive on neglect. The most dangerous enemy of the sansevieria is the over-zealous owner who feels that he or she must be forever watering, watering, watering. Having very thick, fleshy leaves the plant is able to go for long periods without attention.

I was once informed by a lady plant grower that when she purchased her sansevieria the advice given by the supplier was that she should water it once each year in August. On asking her, somewhat incredulously, how long it had lasted under such harsh treatment she replied that it was in its fourth year and doing very well! One would hesitate to offer this as general advice, but it does help to illustrate just how tolerant of dry conditions this plant actually is, and that when watering the tendency should always be to err on the side of dry, rather than wet, compost.

Full light is essential, feeding not particularly important, but reasonable warmth should be provided. A combination of cold and wet conditions can be particularly harmful. Pale green, sweetly scented flowers are sometimes hailed as something of a phenomenon, but older plants will flower quite regularly during the summer months, and even relatively young plants will sometimes oblige. There is always an element of doubt concerning the best time to pot plants on into larger pots, but not with this one as he will happily break the pot in which he is growing when roots and rhizomatous growth become too congested. The plant can then be transferred into a slightly larger clay pot, using J.I.P.3 compost and potting fairly firmly. The reason for the clay pot is that the sansevieria is inclined to be top heavy and the heavier clay pot will help to maintain its equilibrium.

There are a number of other sansevierias that one is likely to come across, all of which require similar treatment. However, *S. t. hahnii* and *S. t.* Golden Hahnii are the only two worthy of mention, both making compact rosettes of overlapping leaves, the one green and the other with yellow-gold colouring. These are extremely slow growing and must be the ideal sort of plant for a bottle garden as there is little chance of them ever becoming overgrown.

SAXIFRAGA SARMENTOSA (Mother of Thousands)

Asia. 10 to 16°C. (50 to 60°F.). Easy.

Very easy to grow, these saxifrages make excellent hanging-basket plants, and are best made up as self baskets so that the young plantlets can be seen to better advantage when they cascade down. The common name is derived from the fact that the plant forms masses of young plantlets in much the same way as strawberries, and can be propagated very simply by removing well-developed young plants and potting them up individually. General care presents few problems, as these plants do perfectly well in most environments where other plants are being grown.

The variegated form *Saxifraga sarmentosa tricolor* is much less vigorous, requiring more 167

careful handling, and will certainly need the higher temperatures indicated above. It will also do better if confined to small pots, as growth is not sufficiently active to justify planting them in hanging baskets as suggested above for the green form.

SCHEFFLERA DIGITATA

New Zealand. 13 to 18°C. (55 to 65°F.). Easy.

As small plants *Schefflera digitata* and its Australian relative *Schefflera actinophylla* are not particularly exciting, but as mature specimens there are few plants with purely green foliage which can match them for elegance. They are easy to manage in light, airy conditions. New plants are usually raised from seed, but hard wood of older plants that have become leggy and unattractive is not difficult to propagate in reasonable conditions.

SCINDAPSUS (Money Plant or Devil's Ivy)

South East Asia. 13 to 18°C. (55 to 65°F.). Difficult and moderately easy.

Of the two common names money plant seems to be by far the most suitable as far as the plant supplier is concerned. On a visit to our nursery some years ago a charming Indian girl, with a surprising knowledge of plants, informed us that in her country the saying went that you would never be without money if you had a scindapsus plant in the house – a good reason for us all to have one.

Belonging to the same family as *Philodendron scandens*, (*Araceae*) the scindapsus has slightly larger but similarly shaped leaves and requires much the same treatment. *Scindapsus aureus* has golden variegated leaves which require careful selection when new plants are being propagated, otherwise they soon revert to an uninteresting green. A moist moss support for plants to climb and get their roots into will greatly improve their performance. Potting compost should be peaty in its composition and the inclusion of a little good leafmould will be an advantage if it can be obtained.

S. aureus Marble Queen is much less robust in its growth and will try the skill of the most experienced of plantsmen. This is mainly on account of the very small amount of chlorophyll in the leaves; some are almost entirely white. To be able to do anything with these plants at all it is essential that they have a temperature in the region of 18°C., and that the pots be plunged in moist peat to their rims – a dry atmosphere can be particularly harmful.

A magnificent specimen of *Ananas bracteatus striatus*, the variegated pineapple. Though rewarding to grow, the sharpness of the saw-toothed leaves suggests that it should be given plenty of space

169

SCHLUMBERGERA (Christmas Cactus)

Brazil. 13 to 18°C. (55 to 65°F.). Easy.

At one time called zygocactus, the correct name is now schlumbergera; the common name of Christmas Cactus will suit most plant growers who are not too deeply interested in nomenclature. Among the easiest of plants to grow, they may be raised from cuttings taken at almost any time of the year provided the pieces chosen do not have flowers on them. Cuttings should be broken off and allowed to dry for a few hours before being inserted up to half a dozen in each $3\frac{1}{2}$-in. pot filled with a peaty compost; a proper cutting mixture is not necessary. Keep the compost moist but never saturated and place the plants out of doors in a sunny corner during the summer, or in a light window at other times. A common complaint is that flower buds drop off before they open for no apparent reason. Fluctuations in temperature or the amount of water given and moving the plant from its light window position as buds are about to open are three good reasons for plants shedding buds prematurely.

SEDUM SIEBOLDII MEDIO-VARIEGATUM

Japan. Hardy. Easy.

Attractive dual-purpose plants that may be grown indoors or planted out in the garden. Adequate light is essential for plants indoors, also reasonable moisture during the summer months – much less at other times. The green form is much less attractive.

SELAGINELLA

Tropics. Minimum 13°C. (55°F.). Difficult.

These compact, moss-like ferns would be difficult to manage in an ordinary room, but they are ideally suited to bottle garden cultivation. They should at no time dry out and the moist, humid atmosphere of the bottle garden or Wardian case should ensure that the proper conditions are maintained. There are a number of varieties available, the majority a pleasant shade of green, but there are others with a decidedly blue tinge which is most attractive. When

potting or propagating it is important that the compost should contain about one third fresh sphagnum moss, to ensure an open mixture. Compost is hardly the word, as the mixture required is nothing more than clean peat and moss. Propagate by cutting pieces of stem and trimming off the lower leaves before inserting in the peat and sphagnum moss mixture; in order to be reasonably successful a temperature of not less than 24°C. (75°F.) should be maintained.

SENECIO MACROGLOSSUS (German Ivy, Cape Ivy)

South Africa. 13 to 18°C. (55 to 65°F.). Easy.

If a small-leaved, quick-growing plant is required this could well be the one. The cream-variegated leaves are roughly triangular in shape, and the plant has a natural clinging habit which will take it to the ceiling in a very short space of time. To prevent growth becoming too long and thin it is wise to provide some form of trellis support round which the plant can be twined. Leaves are fleshy to the touch, but otherwise

resemble those of the smaller hederas, and many is the time we have had flower show visitors come up and whisper that we have made a mistake with one of our labels, only to be assured in an equally low whisper that it isn't an ivy!

Cuttings root very easily at most times of the year and should be inserted several to a small pot filled with standard potting compost. The tips should be removed almost as soon as the young plants show signs of growth to keep the plants much fuller and more attractive at the base. Like the majority of these quick-growing plants it is better to start new ones each year and discard the overgrown parents. Greenfly can be troublesome and is usually found on the young growing tips.

SETCREASEA

Mexico. 10 to 16°C. (50 to 60°F.). Easy.

Of the two that one is likely to come across *Setcreasea striata* has delicately lined pale green leaves, and *S. purpurea* has, as the name suggests, purple colouring. Belonging to the same family 171

Ficus benjamina, the weeping fig (left background), *Dizygotheca elegantissima*, and three of the colourful codiaeums. At the foot of these is *Hedera helix* Adam

Opposite: Placed at the back are *Podocarpus macrophyllus*, the Buddhist pine (left) and *Hedera canariensis*, and in the foreground, chlorophytum (left) and *Schefflera actinophylla*

as the tradescantia, *Commelinaceae*, they are both reasonably easy to care for. *S. purpurea* is the one that the house plant grower is most likely to encounter. It develops into a larger and somewhat untidy plant which flowers quite freely during the summer months. However, untidy growth is never a problem, as the plant can be cut back quite severely at almost any time in order to improve its appearance and prevent it from becoming straggly.

Cuttings resulting from the pruning operation will root with little difficulty in standard potting compost; several pieces should be inserted in each pot.

The colour of this plant will be considerably improved if there is good light, but some protection should be given from strong sunlight. As with almost all the tradescantia tribe saturated compost should be avoided, particularly during the winter months.

SOLANUM CAPSICASTRUM (Winter Cherry)

Brazil. 13 to 18°C. (55 to 65°F.). Easy.

With the increased popularity of the poinsettia at Christmas the solanum has lost much of its appeal. Usual procedure is to purchase these while bearing their red or orange-coloured berries, and to dispose of them when they are no longer attractive. Indoors they require the lightest possible position; in poor light they soon deteriorate. Keep the compost moist and feed with weak liquid fertiliser at regular intervals to keep the foliage a pleasant colour.

Plants can be kept from one year to the next, but it is better to start with new plants. They can be increased from cuttings taken from the old plant in March or April and rooted in warmth in a sandy compost, or from seed sown in February or early March in a temperature of 18°C.

SPARMANNIA (African Wind Flower)

South Africa. September to April 10 to 16°C. (50 to 60°F.), April to September 16 to 21°C. (60 to 70°F.). Easy.

Also known as the indoor lime, *Sparmannia africana* is a rather beautiful plant which is also easy to manage, but one does not see nearly enough of it. Perhaps there is a reluctance on the part of the purchaser that deters the nurseryman from producing them as part of his range. A pity, as they are easily propagated, easy to grow in average conditions indoors, and will adjust to almost any of the temperatures suggested. Where a large plant is required they will develop into substantial size in time, but can equally easily be kept under control by cutting them back to more manageable size. However, it is essential that they should be kept moist all the time, and that feeding should be a regular practice while the plant is in active growth. They will also benefit from annual potting on in early spring using J.I.P.3 compost. Rather than potting plants on and keeping them within bounds by cutting back, it is better to keep them for two or three years and then replace them.

Fresh plants can be started very easily from cuttings which will root at almost any time if conditions are agreeable. White flowers are produced in summer, the pistils of which open outwards at the slightest breath of wind – hence the common name.

SPATHIPHYLLUM (White Sails)

Tropical America. 16 to 21°C. (60 to 70°F.). Moderately easy.

The house plant grower is likely to come across two of these, *Spathiphyllum wallisii* and *S.*

Spathiphyllum wallisii

175

Mauna Loa, the latter being much the scarcer of the two and having generally larger flowers and leaves than the former. Belonging to the *Araceae* family, they require moist, warm and shaded conditions – bright sunlight will quickly drain the rich green colouring from the leaves.

Propagation is by division of the roots, and can be done at almost any time while the plants are not in flower, but preferably in the spring of the year so that the divided pieces can benefit from the more agreeable growing conditions prevailing. For the initial period following division the young plants should be put in small pots filled with a compost composed almost entirely of fresh sphagnum peat. Once they have rooted well into this medium they can be transferred to a more conventional compost, but the emphasis should still be largely on a peat-based mixture. Healthy plants produce a regular succession of creamy white flowers that keep well when cut, so are much in demand by those interested in flower arranging.

STEPHANOTIS FLORIBUNDA
(Madagascar Jasmine)

Madagascar. October to April 10 to 13°C. (50 to 55°F.), April to October 16 to 21°C. (60 to 70°F.). Easy.

The heavily scented wax cluster flowers of this plant make it a particular favourite, and individual 'pips' (flowers) are ever in demand by florists for making up into wedding bouquets. In ideal conditions the growth may even be described as rampant, therefore some form of trellis or other support is essential for the twining growth to attach itself to. If allowed to run, individual stems seem to go on for miles, but it is usually better to restrict them either by pruning or by winding the growth back and forth around itself, which frequently results in the plant flowering more prolifically. Planted in the border or in a large pot in the garden room with growth fanned out against the wall, or overhead, it will give the maximum number of flowers if this is the most important consideration. In this situation it is important that the plant should be lightly shaded and that suggested temperatures are maintained.

During the winter months plants should be kept very much on the dry side, particularly so where the lower temperature is likely to apply. In these conditions plants will almost inevitably lose a number of leaves, but this should not cause too much concern as they quickly refurbish themselves when better spring growing conditions arrive. The reason for keeping the compost only just moist in winter is that wet compost allied to low temperatures can be especially harmful to many indoor plants, and the stephanotis is no exception.

Besides being excellent plants for the garden room, quite unexpected successes are frequently achieved when they are used purely for indoor decoration. Indoors it is most important that plants should have adequate light in which to grow, and that the compost must not become too wet for long periods – permanently saturated compost will result in eventual root failure which in turn will mean the loss of the plant. Flowers are produced over a long period during the spring and summer months, and the owner can find an additional interest by pollinating a few of them. The giant green seed pods of the stephanotis will, indeed, provide a continual source of interest for visitors, but as these will sap the energy of the plant no more than one or two should be allowed to develop.

Mealy bug and scale are two troublesome pests that must be kept in check; particularly so when they are attacking the twining overhead growth of plants in the garden room. Once in 10-in. pots plants can be sustained by regular feeding, but until then they should be potted on every second year into slightly larger pots using J.I.P.3 compost, which should be well firmed but not rammed down hard.

STRELITZIA REGINAE (Bird of Paradise Flower)

South Africa. 13 to 18°C. (55 to 65°F.). Easy.

With its supremely exotic flowers and a name that leaves nothing to be desired one would expect the strelitzia to be one of the most popular of plants, but there is a snag. The snag is that they take three to five years to produce these flowers and there seems to be no way of hastening nature's slow process. So the most limiting factor in their commercial prospects is the time required to raise marketable plants. However, there is no reason why the interested greenhouse or garden-room owner with time to wait for results should not grow them with complete success in conditions that need not be too sophisticated. Raised from seed sown in early spring in John Innes seed sowing compost or similar, they are not difficult to germinate if a temperature in the region of 21°C. (70°F.) can be maintained. Pot progressively into larger pots using J.I.P.3, but do avoid using very large pots out of proportion to the size of the plants; it should be remembered that flowering plants will usually flower much more freely if roots are confined to a smaller area. Plants can also be increased by dividing older specimens and

Opposite:
Scindapsus aureus (left foreground), *Maranta leuconeura kerchoveana*, popularly known as rabbit's tracks, *Peperomia caperata* Little Fantasy (left background), *Aglaonema* Silver Queen (right background), *Hypocyrta glabra*, the orange-flowered clog plant, and in the centre and right foreground, *Fittonia verschaffeltii*

planting them up individually in pots early in the year.

There are other species available, but it should be ensured before acquiring them that they can be expected to flower in reasonable time and that they are not likely to grow too tall. Writing this I have in mind a plant of *S. augusta* that grew to a height of some 15 ft. when confined to a pot and was eventually disposed of in its fourteenth year when it was decided that we could not possibly justify waiting any longer for it to flower. Hence the warning: you may expend a great deal of time and effort and have little or no reward at the end of the day unless you make enquiries first.

STREPTOCARPUS

Central and South America. October to April 7 to 13°C. (45 to 55°F.), April to October 13 to 18°C. (55 to 65°F.). Easy.

Grown from seed or cuttings, these are useful and colourful plants which will flower for many months of the year in the garden room. Seed is sown in February–March in the conventional manner in well-moistened compost. The variety *Streptocarpus* Constant Nymph is an excellent plant producing a succession of violet-blue flowers on slender stems over a long period, and is not in the least difficult to increase in numbers, by inserting complete leaves or leaf sections in peaty compost at a temperature of about 18°C. (65°F.). There is also a white form of this plant which is equally easy to care for. In recent years a number of hybrids have also been developed and there is now a wide colour range to choose from. A lightly shaded position which is also cool and airy should be provided. Feed regularly during the spring and summer and pot on vigorous plants annually using a standard house plant compost which is not too heavy; that is, with a reasonable amount of peat in its make up to prevent it becoming compacted.

STROMANTHE AMABILIS

Brazil. 13 to 18°C. (55 to 65°F.). Moderately easy.

Warm, shaded conditions are required for this low-growing, compact plant. The potting compost should be similar to a mixture of equal parts J.I.P.3 and sphagnum peat, but potting on should only be necessary for vigorous plants every second or third year. These are fine plants for grouping in small indoor gardens. Propagate in warm conditions using pieces of stem with at least two sound leaves attached.

TETRASTIGMA VOINIERIANUM

South East Asia. 16 to 21°C. (60 to 70°F.). Easy.

If you have a wall or trellis that requires to be covered quickly with foliage, then this could well be your plant. In good conditions the growth could be described as rampant, so much so that if a nurseryman grows more than a few dozen larger plants he is almost obliged to have someone permanently posted by the plants in order to tie in the growth as it develops, otherwise it gets out of hand in no time. Nevertheless, it is an effective plant where a bold appearance is needed and is not difficult to manage in reasonable conditions. Shade from direct sunlight and ensure that the compost at no time dries out, also feed regularly when plants are established in their pots. Potting on annually into larger containers is essential, and the compost to use is J.I.P.3. On greenhouse staging or when plants are plunged in beds of peat it will be found that the roots will quickly make their way through the holes in the bottom of the pot. Any potting on following this will entail breaking the pot in order to avoid excessive damage to the root system.

Opposite: *Strelitzia reginae*, the bird of paradise flower

Streptocarpus Constant Nymph

THUNBERGIA ALATA (Black-eyed Susan)

Tropical Africa. 13 to 18°C. (55 to 65°F.). Easy.

Mostly of climbing habit, there are a number of thunbergias that the garden-room owner may well wish to acquire, but Black-eyed Susan is far and away the most popular and, consequently, the variety most likely to be encountered. Plants are not difficult to raise, either from seed sown in the spring of the year, or from cuttings 2 or 3 in. in length taken at the same time and inserted in J.I.P.1 compost. This plant has a certain amount of adaptability in that it may be placed so that growth can be trained to a trellis, or plants may be placed along the edge of the staging to trail over and create an equally good effect. As hanging basket plants they are also attractive, and may be placed out of doors in sheltered areas during the summer months.

TILLANDSIA

Tropical South America. 10 to 21°C. (50 to 70°F.). Easy.

The wide difference in the suggested temperatures will give some indication of the adaptability and tolerance this plant has of varying conditions. There are many different sorts to choose from, all of them compact and easy to care for if the growing conditions are agreeable. All will do

well if attached to a piece of cork bark and suspended from the ceiling of the greenhouse or garden room. First wrap sphagnum moss around the roots, then use plastic-covered wire to bind the plant and moss to the bark. From then on periodic immersion of the plant and bark in a bucket of water seems to be all they require to succeed. In fact, *Tillandsia usneoides* (Spanish moss) will grow perfectly well without compost or moss, simply by draping it over any convenient support. The thread-like foliage is silver-grey in colour and can add considerably to the interest and appearance of a plant collection.

T. cyanea is quite different. It has recurving green foliage, and in time the most exotic bracts appear, pink in colour. From the sides of these bracts petunia-blue flowers are produced in summer over a period of several weeks. To increase plants the clumps are teased apart and individual pieces are planted in peaty compost and subsequently into compost similar to that suggested for bromeliads.

TOLMIEA MENZIESII (Pick-a-back Plant)

North America. 10 to 13°C. (50 to 55°F.). Easy.

Giving a plant an interesting common name can make a deal of difference when the time comes for the nurseryman to dispose of it. This being so it is odd that the commercial grower does not

give more space to producing the pick-a-back plant. As few of them do, one normally has to rely on acquaintances in order to obtain plants. Fortunately this is not difficult as properly formed little plantlets appear all over mature plants of this tolmiea; hence the common name. Cool, light conditions should be provided, and plants are best potted on into larger pots each year. When they become too large and untidy it is best to dispose of them and start with a fresh plant. Plants are hardy out of doors, so temperature is not terribly important, but somewhere in the region of 10°C. (50°F.) should be maintained to keep them in good condition.

TRADESCANTIA (Wandering Sailor)

South America. 7 to 16°C. (45 to 60°F.). Easy.

Also known as Wandering Jew, there are many delightful tradescantias that can be put to many uses, and most of them are as tough as old boots.

Light and airy conditions suit them best; in restricted light there will be a marked tendency for the attractively variegated foliage to turn green and lose its appearance. Plants are available in many colours, including gold and pink, but silver is the most popular and the striking silver foliage of *Tradescantia* Quicksilver is probably the best. All of them grow very easily from cuttings a few inches in length, and it is best to renew plants each year. When striking cuttings, five or six pieces should be placed in a small pot filled with J.I.P.2 compost, and when they have begun to grow the leading growths ought to be pinched out so that branching growth and more attractive plants develop.

In the garden room tradescantias make superb hanging baskets, which are best planted up in early March. Place at least five plants in each basket and pin the growth in to the side of the basket as it develops so that a complete ball of colour is produced. We are often advised that tradescantias should be kept dry and no fertiliser

should be given in order to maintain the colourful variegation. This advice is a lot of eyewash as plants, particularly in hanging baskets, will do infinitely better if they are kept moist and regularly fed. Any purely green growth that may appear must be removed, otherwise the faster growing green shoots in the basket will rapidly take over.

Besides the more usual tradescantias there are a number that one comes across only occasionally. Among these is *T. blossfeldiana* with leaves which are more fleshy and also hairy. There is also a slower growing variegated form with cream and green markings; named *T. blossfeldiana tricolor*, it is a little more difficult to manage, but a fine plant when well grown. The first mentioned of these two is a particularly tough plant which seems to withstand all sorts of ill treatment and fares better under these conditions than when being fussed over all the time.

In conditions where the temperature of 16°C.

(60°F.) suggested above can be maintained *T. reginae* could be tried. This is a much more delicate plant suitable only for the more experienced plant grower with favourable conditions. Growth is more erect with silver and green leaves which are purple underneath and fully 6 in. in length. Warmth, humidity and lightly shaded conditions should be provided if this plant is to succeed.

VRIESIA

Tropical South America. 16 to 21°C. (60 to 70°F.). Moderately easy.

Among these members of the bromeliad family are some of the most majestic of plants, some of which are only suitable where adequate space is available. For example, *Vriesia imperialis* will in time develop rosettes of leaves, pale green in colour, which are over 4 ft. in diameter. As the name suggests, *V. fenestralis* has delicately 183

Vriesia splendens

patterned leaves and producing plants with unblemished leaves will test the skill of the most accomplished plantsman. *V. hieroglyphica* is very similar in shape to the previous one, but the interest here is in the black and green bands of colour. All the foregoing will take many years before they produce bracts when grown from seed, but their attractive foliage makes them well worth trying.

Far and away the most popular is *V. splendens*, which is reasonably small and compact and much more practical for the commercial nursery-man to handle. Leaves have broad bands of light and dark green which make them attractive in themselves, but the principal feature is the spear-shaped red bract that may be two or more feet in length and remains colourful for many months on end. Flowers that appear along each side of the bract are yellow in colour, but not particularly attractive. When purchasing plants one should choose them before the stage at which they are producing flowers. It is odd, but as the bract develops the dual-coloured leaves lose this interest and become plain green. After flowering the bract and the rosette from which it appeared will die back quite naturally and new young plants will be produced at the base of the parent rosette. These may be treated in the same way as recommended for the aechmea.

All the vriesias have leaves which form natural vases for holding water which should not be allowed to dry out. The compost in the pot need be kept only just moist, and will need very little water during the winter months. It is usually better not to feed bromeliads as feeding with specially prepared house plant fertilisers can often damage the leaves.

ZEBRINA PENDULA

Mexico. 10 to 16°C. (50 to 60°F.). Easy.

The treatment here is almost identical to that advised for the tradescantia, and zebrinas are equally easy to manage. Plants may be grown at lower temperatures than that advised, but in cooler conditions the foliage becomes very hard in appearance and is much less attractive. Leaves are dark green and brown and have a touch of silver in them that seems to sparkle in healthy plants; undersides of leaves are purple.

These are excellent plants for hanging baskets, either as individual subjects or when incorporated with other plants. Cuttings a few inches in length root with little trouble and can be put directly into the small pots in which they are to be grown using J.I.P.2 compost. Five or six cuttings to a $3\frac{1}{2}$-in. pot will provide plants in no time at all.

Index

Abbreviation: p = photograph

189

Acknowledgements

Most of the colour photographs in this book are by Ernest Crowson, whom we should like to thank. We are also grateful to Pat Brindley and Harry Smith, who contributed the colour photographs on pages 104 and 164, and to Aspect Picture Library for the use of their photograph on page 34.

For the black and white photographs we should like to thank *Amateur Gardening*, Pat Brindley, Robert Corbin, Ernest Crowson, Leslie Johns, Thomas Rochford and Sons Ltd., and Chaloner Woods.

Our thanks also go to Mr and Mrs Joy for allowing us to take photographs in their home, and to Thomas Rochford and Sons Ltd. for providing us with facilities for photography at their house plant nursery.

Coleus